T0338825

Cristòfol Despuig
Dialogues

Cristòfol Despuig Dialogues

A Catalan Renaissance Colloquy Set in the City of Tortosa

Introduction by
Enric Querol and Josep Solervicens

Translation by
Henry Ettinghausen

BARCINO·TAMESIS
BARCELONA/WOODBRIDGE 2014

First published 2014
by Tamesis (Serie B: TEXTOS, 57)
in association with Editorial Barcino

LLLL institut
ramon llull
Catalan Language and Culture

The translation of this work has been supported
by a grant from the Institut Ramon Llull

ISBN 978 1 85566 2 759
COPYRIGHT DEPOSIT: B. 2.552-2014

Tamesis is an imprint of Boydell & Brewer Ltd
PO Box 9, Woodbridge, Suffolk IP12 3DF, UK
and of Boydell & Brewer Inc.
668 Mt Hope Avenue, Rochester, NY 14620, USA
www.boydellandbrewer.com

Editorial Barcino, S. A.
Acàcies 15. 08027 Barcelona, Spain
www.editorialbarcino.cat

Designed and typeset by Jordi Casas

Printed in Spain by Gràfiko

Cover illustration:
Antoni Casanova, *The Emperor Charles V and Titian*
Detail. Oil on canvas, 1878
© Ajuntament de Tortosa, 2014

Contents

Introduction

THE *DIALOGUES* WRITTEN by Cristòfol Despuig[1] in 1557 under the title *Los col·loquis de la insigne ciutat de Tortosa* offer a critical review of a host of issues that were topical at the time. The three speakers in the work — Livio, the knight from Tortosa; Fabio, the gentleman from Tortosa; and Don Pedro, the knight from Valencia — elegantly exchange their subtly contrasting views regarding politics, society and the Church as they stroll through the streets of Tortosa and sail along the Ebro. The main features of the dialogue, which typify the revival of the genre in the Renaissance, lie in the way it expresses differing opinions, creates multiple perspectives and constructs a consistent plot that imitates a spontaneous conversation whilst providing a structure for the speakers' reflections. Both the ways in which it articulates the discussion and the specific ideas that it allocates to its speakers make of Despuig's *Dialogues* a text that exemplifies the Renaissance in Catalonia.

THE AUTHOR

Cristòfol Despuig came from a family that belonged to the minor nobility within the oligarchy of the city of Tortosa. Both in the text of the *Dialogues* and in a non-fictional document, namely his will, it is said that the Tortosa branch of the family was descended from the knight Roger Despuig. That supposed hero of the conquest of Tortosa from the

---

[1] It may be helpful to know that in Catalan Despuig is pronounced "Despooch."

Moors, it was claimed, was one of the four men who scaled the walls of the castle of La Suda on the last day of the year 1148. As a reward, Count Ramon Berenguer IV of Barcelona gave him the house that was to become the family seat in La Rosa Street, as well as the tower of Llaber outside the city walls, and the barony of Paüls on the slopes of El Port. However, no trace of Roger Despuig has ever come to light in the archives, and for the present his existence must be regarded as legendary. On the other hand, Despuigs are documented in Tortosa practically from the moment it was recovered by the Christians — in particular, as lords of Paüls, from the year 1228. The family was connected by marriage to the Bruscas, the lords of Ortells, in the region of Els Ports, and for family reasons the branch of the barons of Paüls came to be known as the Brusca-Despuigs. In 1482 Miquel de Brusca sold the fief to Bartomeu de Viu, a squire resident in Casp, thus putting an end to the ascendancy of the Despuigs.

Another genealogical detail that requires elucidation is the connection between the Despuigs of Tortosa and those of Xàtiva. In the *Dialogues* Pere Despuig, Cristòfol's grandfather, is described as a nephew of Lluís Despuig, the famous Master of the Order of Montesa, who is said to have put him in charge of the fortress of Peniscola during the Catalan civil war. Archival sources bear out this connection. In May 1473 Pere Despuig is documented as bailiff of Peniscola castle, and in the 1470s he appears on several occasions as a proxy for Lluís Despuig. Apart from this well attested relationship, we have also tracked down another point of contact between them. In 1458 Jaume Samboy, *alias* Despuig, a native of Xàtiva, who could well have been a nephew of Lluís Despuig, the Master of Montesa, was put forward by Pere Despuig, Cristòfol's grandfather, for a church benefice of which he was patron. However, that connection still calls for further clarification.

Cristòfol Despuig was born in Tortosa on 10 November 1510, the son of Pere Joan Despuig, sheriff of the city from 1506 to 1508, and Francina Savartès. His grandfather, Pere Despuig, mentioned above, was influential in Tortosa society and became one of the king's strong men in the city on its capitulation to John II in 1466. Apart from his birth, the first mention we find of our author dates from 1522, when he was granted minor orders at the bishop's palace as a "*scolarem litteratum*". Such ordinations were quite common amongst students, because they enabled them to opt for a career in the church and for the rents of benefices, without committing themselves to remain in the clergy. We then move

on to 1530, when Cristòfol marries Maciana Curto i Oliver, whose family also belonged to the oligarchy of Tortosa, thus becoming a relative of
Lluís Oliver de Boteller, the powerful viscount of Castellbò. It is quite
possible that between those two dates, 1522 and 1530, Cristòfol resided
in the palace of the Montcadas in Valencia, like Livio in the *Dialogues*,
who states: "I was educated [...] in the house of a gentleman who was as
courteous and noble in his ways as any within the entire kingdom."

The link to the viscount of Castellbò turned out to be crucial in
Cristòfol's career. Aligned with the Oliver de Boteller party, he became
one of the most important players within the local Tortosa feuds. In
January 1532 the king's constable, Pere-Pau Amat de Palou, went to
Tortosa to put an end to the state of civil war that had taken hold of the
city. On that occasion Despuig was forced to swear allegiance and was
held under house arrest. The following year the situation in the city had
become one of "open warfare": the faction of the Sevil de Canyissars,
Amics and Valls had had to cut off Genoa Street with barricades and
artillery pieces in order to defend itself against "Cristòfol *Puig* and his
friends and protectors" who had hired armed men in their attempt to
storm the house of Pere-Joan Sevil de Canyissar, lord of Paüls, thus
breaching the truce agreed the previous year. In 1533 Despuig spread
panic when a party of a hundred armed men entered the city. Finally, in
1535, the governor of Catalonia forbade him to play any part in the city's
government. However, the flame of dissent was not dampened down
until the arrival of Francesc de Borja as the new viceroy of Catalonia in
1539. He managed to put the Oliver de Botellers on trial, and they were
banished from Catalonia, though they sought refuge in Peniscola castle,
where they held the office of governors, and from there they continued
to exercise control over their interests in Tortosa.

A more peaceful and productive period thus began during which
Despuig became deeply involved in the governance of the city, exercising
the offices of chief procurator, justice in chief — he was president of the
law court — and captain of one of Tortosa's citizens' militias. He was also
a member of several commissions of the town council, including those set
up to construct irrigation channels, to advise the elected representatives
of the city in the Corts, or Parliament, and to oversee public health. In
addition, he acted as municipal delegate in connection with various matters that involved negotiating with Master Gil de Morlanes, in Saragossa,
over the construction of the irrigation scheme, with the Master of
Montesa in order to improve the preparedness of coastal defences

around Sant Jordi d'Alfama, and with the Abbot of Benifassà, Jeroni Sans, and Bishop Ferran de Loaces, with a view to persuading the latter to contribute to the cost of the building works being carried out in the cathedral, as his duty demanded. This last episode, which is reflected in Despuig's first Dialogue, where the bishop is depicted in a rather poor light, brought upon him the enmity of the prelate, who did his best to pressure and discredit him. Given Loaces' powerful influence over the Crown and the Inquisition, that confrontation may well have been a factor in preventing the *Dialogues'* publication at the time.

Early in the 1560s another incident brought about a renewal or revival of hostilities. On 6 December 1563, as they were strolling through the city, Cristòfol Despuig, Francesc Cerdà and Pau Terçà — the son of Miquel Terçà, head of the council of Aragon — were attacked and shot at with a blunderbuss, whereupon the undersheriff, Miquel Esteve, had to call out the militia in order to detain the perpetrators. On 22 December a truce was signed between Jaume Cerveró, archdeacon of Corbera, the chamberlain Mateu Boteller, Pere Boteller, Joan Moliner, Gaspar Jordà, Joan Canyissar de Sevil, lord of Paüls, Pere-Josep Sevil and Francesc Sevil, on the one hand, and Cristòfol Despuig, canon Onofre Despuig, his son, Tomàs Costa, canon and abbot of Sant Serni de Tavèrnoles, Cristòfol Costa, Francesc Cerdà and the brothers Pau and Jaume Terçà, on the other—the cream of the local nobility. For reasons that are still unclear, on that occasion Despuig appears to have been at odds with the Oliver de Boteller faction. The latter enjoyed the powerful protection of Pere Oliver de Boteller, lieutenant Inquisitor of the district of Tortosa, who took under his wing the gangs of malefactors who operated in the service of his family clan. With a view to teaching their opponents a lesson, the Despuigs, father and son, got their hired assassins to set fire to the house of Cosme Castellar, constable of the Inquisition. The Holy Office, for its part, decided that this constituted an attack on the institution itself and took action. In 1565 Onofre was imprisoned in the Inquisition cells in Valencia, and Cristòfol was held under house arrest, but the situation changed unexpectedly when, on 9 August 1566, the Inquisitors of Valencia wrote to the Tortosa Chapter to inform them of the death, in unspecified circumstances, of Onofre Despuig.

The case was followed at Court with concern. The viceroys of Valencia and Catalonia were told on several occasions to keep tight control over Francesc Moliner and Cristòfol Despuig and were ordered to prevent them going to live in Tortosa under any circumstances. It would appear that our author spent the years of banishment in Barcelona, Valencia and Traiguera, whilst his wife took care of the family assets from Tortosa. The death of Moliner enabled Cristòfol to ask for permission to return, and on 27 March 1571, taking note of the positive reports of Viceroy Hernando de Toledo and the bishop of Tortosa, the king granted him the favour he sought. Despuig once again took his place in the social and economic life of Tortosa, managing the rents from the two bakeries he owned; acting as head of the noble confraternity, the Brotherhood of Saint George, in 1572/73; and — to the consternation of the canons, who objected to its excessive pomp — beginning the construction of a sumptuous tomb for himself in the chapel of the Immaculate Conception in the cathedral, of which he was a patron by virtue of a bequest received from the Macip family. On 7 August 1574, just a few days before his death, he dictated his last will and testament, in which he named his grandson Pau-Martí Corder his sole heir, on condition that he change his surname to Despuig and become a knight, which he did in 1592, when he and his brother Dionís petitioned the council of Aragon.

CULTURAL LIFE IN TORTOSA

In Cristòfol Despuig's day, Tortosa was, demographically and economically, one of the most flourishing cities in Catalonia, capable of keeping up with the intellectual and literary developments and the cultural innovations of the time. In the first place, due to its geographical position, the city enjoyed a close relationship with the great cultural centres of the Crown of Aragon — with Saragossa, with which it had strong commercial links, thanks to navigation along the Ebro; with Aragon in general, from which it received large numbers of clergy, schoolmasters, choirmasters and other lettered professionals; and with Valencia, because the diocese of Tortosa stretched as far as Almenara, only thirty kilometres from that city, which acted as a powerful magnet for professional men from Tortosa. Besides, the bishop and the chapter of Tortosa cathedral were closely involved in Valencian politics by virtue of their electability to the ecclesiastical arm of the standing commission of the Valencian Generalitat, or Parliamentary Estates. Thus, questions of strictly Valencian interest, such as how to assimilate the Moorish minority, were necessarily subject to the views of the clergy of Tortosa.

Finally, Barcelona represented a higher stage for the professional and political aspirations of the men of Tortosa, and they committed themselves wholeheartedly to the government of the principality through the Catalan Generalitat, with families such as the Oliver de Botellers and the Jordàs playing important roles at the forefront of the institution. They were also prominent in the Royal High Court, a key centre of power coveted by jurists, and in Barcelona University. In addition, individual and social connections, reinforced by family links, connected Tortosans to places that, whilst they carried less political weight, were important from a cultural point of view, such as Lleida, Morella, Sant Mateu, Alcanyís and the Cistercian monastery of Benifassà. The latter, located in the Valencian zone of the diocese, was run largely by monks from Tortosa and possessed a sizeable part of its estate in the Ebro region.

Besides these geopolitical considerations, Tortosa had cultural institutions that proved decisive when it came to assimilating and spreading knowledge, such as the city's grammar school and the Dominican university, where lay people could study the arts and theology as early as 1530. Nevertheless, it also suffered from some serious shortcomings for intellectual development. Even though Niccolò Perotti's *Rudimenta grammatices* were printed in Tortosa in 1477, and the typographer Arnau Guillem de Montpesat was active there in 1538/39, the printing press — with all it meant as a stimulus and promoter of literary production — did not become properly established in the city until 1622. At the same time, the Aristotelian-Thomistic orientation of its Royal Colleges, as well as Inquisitorial pressures, proved to be negative forces when it came to promoting humanism and a critical spirit.

Despuig belongs to the first generation educated in good humanistic Latin and familiar with the Erasmian ideas that spread throughout Europe, and in particular throughout Spain, up to the time of Erasmus' death in 1536. Teachers clearly inspired by the new grammatical and intellectual approaches, such as Daniel Sisó and Jeroni Amiguet, had been masters at Tortosa's grammar school. After Despuig attended it, we find that other important teachers were Joan Franch, who taught Palmireno, the Valencian Erasmist Francesc Deci, and the neo-Latin poet from Alcanyís, Domingo Andrés. However, the state of education in the city should not be exaggerated. In Despuig's day we do not find a great host of literary figures, as we do at the end of the sixteenth century, with authors such as Jeroni d'Herèdia, Joan Dessí, Juan Suárez de

Godoy and Francesc Vicent Garcia. Amongst Despuig's contemporaries we can count the Dominican Baltasar Sorió, who founded the Royal Colleges and left numerous writings, including books of sermons, apologetic and theological tracts, and even a Christmas eclogue that was performed at the monastery of Sant Mateu. We also find Tortosa-born Jeroni Taix, who wrote the *Libre del Roser*, a genuine sixteenth-century best seller that was continuously reprinted well into the eighteenth century. However, those theologians are far removed from Despuig's interests, as too was Bartomeu Cucala, from Sant Mateu, the author of *Baculus clericalis* (Valencia, 1524), a manual for the education of the clergy that was translated into Spanish in 1539 and was also a commercial success.

A good deal more interesting from a humanistic point of view is Cosme Violaigua, a monk from Benifassà and Master of Theology, who oversaw an edition of Vives' dialogues — *Epicedion super morte clariss. viri Ludovici Vives*— that was printed in Valencia some time between 1540 and 1554, preceded by elegiac verses penned by various personalities from Valencia and Benifassà. Violaigua acted as representative of the Tortosa chapter before Philip II when it was at odds with Bishop Loaces, an affair in which, as we have seen, Despuig too played a prominent role. Violaigua also wrote poems that preface Francesc Deci's prayer *Patribus iuratis pro numere oratorio musas* (Valencia, 1549) and Jeroni Sempere's *Libro de cavallería celestial del pie de la rosa fragante* (Antwerp, 1554), which link him to Valencian university and poetic circles of the mid-sixteenth century. The learned Jeroni Sans also lived at Benifassà, where he was abbot from 1532 until his death in 1554, and Despuig makes direct reference to him in several passages of the *Dialogues*. Amongst other works, Sans wrote *Aragonum clara insignia regum*, now lost, a genealogy of the Aragonese royal house dedicated to the deputy chancellor, Miquel Mai, and a *Crónica del rey don Juan de Aragón* (Valencia, 1541), based on the works of Lucio Marineo Sículo. In the field of historiography we have the Alcanyís jurist and antiquary Alonso Gutiérrez, who, in about 1540, wrote the earliest known essay on the history of his town, *Memorias y antigüedades de Alcañiz,* although it was not published at the time. Gutiérrez, who was married to Tortosa-born Àngela d'Icart and spent lengthy periods in the city, where he had a house, doubtless provided a stimulus to the local intelligentsia.

Another person worth taking note of when comparing the cultural scene in Valencia and in Catalonia is Marc-Antoni d'Aldana (1529-1591), the son of Joan d'Aldana, the hero of the battle of Pavia, and a brother of Anníbal d'Aldana, who married Despuig's daughter Anna. Marc-Antoni's dealings with Despuig went beyond the bare minimum of family connections, as can be seen from the fact that, during the trouble the Despuigs had with the Inquisition in 1564/65, Marc-Antoni wrote to the Inquisitors of Valencia in support of the Despuigs' conduct. Little is known of Marc-Antoni d'Aldana's literary works, and he has frequently been confused with the poet Francisco de Aldana, known as *El Divino*, but one sonnet by him appears at the beginning of the *Primera parte de la carolea* (Valencia, 1560), and another in the *Història del regne de Mallorca* — written by Joan Binimelis in Catalan in 1595, and in Spanish in 1601 — which remained unpublished at the time. Another of his compositions appears amongst the laudatory poems that accompany the *Discursos, epístolas y epigramas de Artemidoro* (Saragossa, 1605) of Andrés Rey de Artieda, who also belonged to the Valencian literary fraternity. Within the family circle we also come across the jurist Joan Amic, editor of the *Libre de les Costums generals escrites de la ciutat de Tortosa* (Tortosa, 1539), whose sister had married Joan d'Aldana.

On the other hand, we have no evidence that Despuig was in touch with scholars from the region who were not resident in Tortosa, such as the Hellenist Cosme de Palma, from Sant Mateu, the well-known heretic Pere Galès, from Ulldecona, or the humanist Pere Lluís Berga, from La Jana or possibly from Sant Mateu, all of whom were clearly occupied by spiritual and intellectual concerns and came to differing ends. Palma studied at Louvain, took part in meetings of the Spanish group at the University there that showed marked Lutheran tendencies, and ended up denouncing the coterie to the authorities. Once installed in orthodoxy, his brilliant career as a theologian enabled him to take part in the Council of Trent, after which, having gained favour with the king, he spent his last years translating Greek and Latin codices in the library of the Escorial. Galès, for his part, a pupil of the Hellenist Pere Joan Núñez, also achieved great prestige as a humanist. However, fearful of the repressive atmosphere in Spain, he spent an itinerant life as a teacher in Italy, Switzerland and France, though he ended up dying in the Inquisition jail in Saragossa in 1595. Berga, a disciple of Peter Ramus and Juan Pérez de Pineda in Paris, became involved with the Protestant circle in Pedralba led by Serafí de Centelles. Accused of Lutheranism, he was burned in effigy in 1572, although nothing is known for certain about his personal fate. These characters illustrate the dangers involved in too openly adopting attitudes favourable to the Reformation or

Erasmianism. They also demonstrate the need to justify or play down criticism that we find reflected throughout the *Dialogues* — the dissemblance required for survival.

Despuig took part in the process of rescuing Classical texts, concepts and styles of writing begun by the Renaissance in Italy, a process in which educated people around him played varying roles, assimilating the literary novelties to differing extents. The *Dialogues*, the only literary text he wrote, appear, then, not as the work of a lone scholar, but — both in its themes and its choice of genre — as the logical creation of a writer of his time.

THE USE OF DIALOGUE: CHARACTERS, FRAMEWORK AND STRUCTURE

Dialogue is one of the Classical genres reclaimed by the Renaissance, which turns it into a hallmark of the period. To name but a few of those who adopted the genre and undoubtedly moulded Renaissance thought, we need only think of Pontanus, Bembo, Machiavelli, Erasmus, Castiglione, Valdés, Minturno, Speroni, Patrizi or Tasso. Dialogue is an argumentative genre that is especially appropriate for reflecting on philosophical, artistic and political propositions and thinking about everyday reality. It does so by using fictional means, by way of speakers, a setting and a plot. In the Catalan-speaking world nearly forty dialogues were written in the course of the Renaissance. Despuig's *Dialogues* stand out from the rest by the extent to which they incorporate the most innovative aspects of the genre: the dramatisation of Renaissance multiple perspectives and the consistency of the fictional plot that provides a structure for the ideas.

The *Dialogues* are presented in the form of six micro-dialogues that have three speakers as their protagonists. Livio is a knight from Tortosa who is educated, has a critical and inquisitive mind, and is cosmopolitan, bold and ironical. His is the most critical voice in the work: he protests about the Castilianisation of the Catalan nobility, questions the credibility of miracles, justifies Philip II's actions against the Papal States, and denounces the bishop of Tortosa's avarice, and the lack of independence shown by the city's elected representatives. Fabio, on the other hand, a gentleman involved in Tortosa's local government, is conservative, devout and conformist. He too is an educated person, but he lacks a broad view of life that might have enabled him to evaluate and question the facts he knows and to work out ideas of his own. Don Pedro, the third speaker, is a knight from Valencia who stops off in Tortosa on his way to Barcelona. He is measured, generous and diplomatic, worried about the fate of the Catalan language in Valencia and by the lack of respect accorded to religious affairs, and he defends the privileges of the nobility.

The elegant debates engaged in by the three speakers take place in an ever-changing urban setting: the streets of Tortosa, the interior of the cathedral, the river Ebro. These fictional scenes are created by the hints that the speakers offer us as they stroll about, catch sight of new visual markers, register surprise or make mental connections. They themselves repeatedly make explicit the dual process of walking and talking: "And now, let's go onto the bridge, and we can keep on talking as we walk. There we'll be out in the open", an expression connected to micro-dialogue 22 of the colloquy *Linguae latinae exercitatio* by the Valencian humanist Joan Lluís Vives: "*Ne assideamus, sed deambulantes colloquamur.*"[2] In fact, the itinerary that Vives traces through early sixteenth-century Valencia in his micro-dialogue has a lot in common with the route that Despuig creates in his *Dialogues,* although Vives uses his fiction in order to teach his readers Latin vocabulary, and not, like Despuig, as a starting point for debate.

In the *Dialogues* there is no narrator to describe the urban setting. It is the speakers who make it visible as they convey their visual impressions of the people who walk about the streets of Tortosa or do business there, recording the greetings and farewells that mark the appearance and disappearance of the characters, the precise topographical features that indicate the locations through which they pass or wish to go, and the detailed allusions to the appearance, clothes and gestures of the people they see as they walk along. The openness of the dialogue suggests the dynamic nature of the urban setting, with Livio recognising Don Pedro across the street through the milling crowd. This sense of movement is essential for understanding not just the openness, but the entire plot, of the work.

The speakers' observations create the illusion of complicity between them, of the intimacy and the confidentiality that they maintain. They speak in a relaxed atmosphere that is enhanced by formulae that are typical of spontaneous conversation, such as jokes and digressions — on the

---

[2] I.e. "Let's not sit down, let's talk as we walk."

hostels of ill repute situated outside the city walls, the benefits of sport, etc. — colloquialisms, popular sayings, diminutives, interruptions, exclamations and oral syntax, and with the redundancies and ellipses that are characteristic of conversational mimesis.

The fictional setting also plays an important part in introducing the topics of conversation and in structuring the dialogue. The fact that we come upon Don Pedro bargaining is not disconnected from the debate on the need for knights to do business with merchants. Nor is the fact that all three speakers describe the flora and the fauna in the lower Ebro valley as they sail and fish in the river. The fiction brings to life the topics on which the speakers reflect, and it also structures them. The characters start a subject off, leave it in suspense, touch on a different one, go back to the first and, before deciding that they have finished with it, set off on a third, without following any obvious logical order. All the same, one of the dialogue's great merits lies precisely in the way the various topics knit into one another. The plot involves a spectacle that covers two days, from Don Pedro's unexpected arrival in Tortosa until he leaves to continue on his way to Barcelona, and it provides the structural axis for the discussions, because the speakers relate the topics they debate as much to what they see before them as to their personal vicissitudes.

The first topic of the *Dialogues*, the state of the Catalan language in Valencia and, by extension, in the entire linguistic area, is determined by the unexpected presence of a Valencian in the principality. The pleasure that Don Pedro derives from coming back to "our ancient native land" sets off the debate. Once the linguistic situation has been discussed, the fiction is made to introduce a new argument. Fabio starts making conjectures about a merchant who is walking along the street, and Don Pedro explains how, just a little earlier, he had been negotiating a credit, so that the discussion is spontaneously set up regarding the relations between knights and merchants. That is to say: the first topic does not give way to the second by reason of a development in the discussion but by a change in the plot. After which, criticism of the bishop is introduced by moving the action on to Tortosa cathedral, to the construction of which he is said not to be contributing enough. Once inside the cathedral, the remains of a twelfth-century church spark off a discussion about belief in relics: relics are the remains of things past (as in the case of the church that they see before them), but — exploiting the kind of mental twist that typifies dialogue — they can also be the body or the clothes of a saint, the ultimate subject of the conversation.

Likewise, at the beginning of the second dialogue, the gastronomic comments prompted by a good lunch lead to a discussion on the change of meaning undergone by the expression "like a Barcelona dinner table", and that gives way to reflections on the falsification and misrepresentation of history by Castilian historians and royal chroniclers. When, in the third Dialogue, the speakers catch sight of "those knights just coming over towards us," and speak to them, the subject of the conversation turns upon the privileges and freedoms granted by Ramon Berenguer IV to the knights who took part in the conquest of Tortosa. And, when they decide to pay a visit to Dona Joana, a lady of Tortosa, what they talk about is the legend of the courageous women of the city and their social rank. In the fourth Dialogue the urban improvements that they notice as they stroll along dispose them to reflect on the need to maintain them by means of good public conduct. When their walk brings them to the Bridge of Boats, by the banks of the Ebro, the speakers stop to read the modern epigram that commemorates its construction, in which the Latin name of the city, Dertosa, appears, and that inspires thoughts about the Classical remains in the city that can still be seen.

The itinerary of the fourth Dialogue ends on the evening of the first day in front of the bridge that crosses the Ebro. Here a new subject of conversation is proposed, this time only seemingly historical, namely the war between the Generalitat and King John II, but it is broken off straight away because there is "a crowd of people" by the bridge, which makes our speakers decide to opt for a quieter and less public place. As for the fifth Dialogue, it is the only one that takes place in an enclosed space, namely a room in Livio's house that keeps them clear of interference from outside, a fact that needs to be seen in the context of the importance of this dialogue's subject. Finally, the sixth Dialogue, the description of the natural resources of the lower Ebro, takes place as the speakers take a trip down river.

TOPICS AND IDEAS

Whilst making use of historical data as the basis for their discussions, the topics on which the speakers reflect have to do with life in their time: the state of the Catalan language, the place of the Crown of Aragon within Spain, Church politics, relations between the social classes, the municipal government of Tortosa, and the fauna and flora on the lands bordering the Ebro. However, the speakers do not spell out a history of the Catalan language. Instead, they talk about the state of the language in the sixteenth century, its loss of prestige, the increasing use of Castilian amongst the nobility and the application of various different names — Limousin, Catalan, Valencian — to one and the same language. Instead of setting out a potted history of Catalonia, they deal with the situation of the Crown of Aragon in the Spain of their day, making use of historical arguments to point out the differences between reality as the law saw it (i.e. political compromise) and reality as it actually was (namely, the progressive subordination of the Crown of Aragon to Castile). Far from reflecting upon spiritual questions, they highlight the contradictions raised by competition between spiritual and temporal power in the figure of Pope Paul IV, the war between Spain and the Papal States for the control of Naples, the scarcely charitable attitudes of the bishop of Tortosa, and belief in miracles and relics. Rather than explain the class or institutional structure of sixteenth-century society, they set out a series of burning questions of the time regarding the relationship between the nobility, the patricians and the merchants — the fact that a nobleman may indulge in commercial affairs, the conceit on the part of merchants who think they can make their trademarks the equivalent of coats of arms, the different kinds of education that ought to be afforded to a young aristocrat or to the son of a merchant, etc. Nor do they simply make out an inventory of the flora and fauna on the banks of the Ebro, but question, instead, the lack of initiatives to exploit its natural resources: mining, the development of an iron industry, overcoming the private interests that prevented the construction of an irrigation scheme. According to Livio, the reason why large-scale reforms are not being carried out lies in the control exercised by the patricians over the municipal government and their concern only for short-term profit.

These are subjects about which there is no absolute truth. The speakers simply give their opinions, defining their contributions by expressions such as "offering an opinion", "believing", "considering", "depending on", "saying what I think" or "giving reasons why", or by actually observing, for instance: "I trust that neither of you will hesitate to contradict me at any point." It is Livio who comes up with the most important opinions and the most striking attitudes in the debates, but all three speakers put forward information and views that acquire validity simply by virtue of the coherence of the arguments they are capable of articulating, without any of the three imposing their authority on the others. In that sense, they may be said to enjoy a 'horizontal relationship'. Instead of dealing with universal truths, about which they could offer certainty, they discuss concrete realities, on which they have differing views, in line with the most complex dialogues of the Renaissance. The controversies over the feasibility of slowing down the adoption of Spanish by the Catalan nobility, or the belief in miracles and relics, both included in the first Dialogue, are fine examples of the multiple perspectives opened up by the genre. Despuig provides the elements needed for the reader to arrive at a complex view of reality by means of the richness of the nuances and the absence of dogmatism that the text is capable of carrying.

The political ideas in the *Dialogues* are its most important and extensive thematic feature. The evocation and narration of historical events acquire a symbolic function, powering the defence of Catalan rights in the face of the self-seeking tendency to confuse the Crown of Castile with Spain. That is why, in the second Dialogue, Livio spells out a veritable counter-history that stresses the heroism of numerous Catalan monarchs and noblemen whose deeds have been forgotten or misrepresented in the histories of Spain written in Castile or promoted by the royal chroniclers. The historian Juan Sedeño, in his *Summa de varones ilustres* (1551), leaves out figures such as James I, Peter the Great, Alfonso the Magnanimous and Ramon Berenguer IV; the imperial chronicler Pedro Mexía, in his *Historia imperial y cesárea* (1545), ascribes the kingdom of Naples to the Crown of Castile, not the Crown of Aragon, and skates over the role played by Ramon Berenguer III in elucidating the innocence of a legendary empress of Germany; whilst another imperial chronicler, Florián de Ocampo, in his *Crónica general de España* (1543), treats Philip of Castile as king of the whole of Spain and locates the first settlement supposedly founded in the Peninsula by Tubal in Andalusia, rather than on the Catalan coast. Livio explains such omissions and distortions as resulting from the expansionist spirit of the Crown of Castile, determined to white out the heroic deeds of the Catalans. However, the speakers' sharp rhetoric is not used in order to reinforce a set of legendary or historical facts, but to dispel the biased confusion between Castile and the whole of Spain and to vindicate the role played at the time by the Crown of Aragon, claiming the same rights for Aragon as for the Crown of Castile, both being "nations of Spain". The account of the war against John II, which takes up the whole of the fifth Dialogue, also has a strong political intent, turning as it does into a consideration that is powerfully linked to the present, with its clear warning of the need to defend the constitutions and to respect treaties, whilst basing those arguments on events that had occurred in the fifteenth century.

In the first Dialogue the definition of the lands where Catalan is spoken and the basis for their linguistic unity, namely those conquered by James I and Alfonso III, implicitly contradict the position defended by Pere Antoni Beuter and Lucio Marineo. The speakers repeat the expression "Catalan language" fifteen times, thus underlining its unity in the face of the terms 'Limousin' and 'Valencian' that Beuter had used to describe one and the same language in his *Crónica general de España y especialmente del Reino de Valencia* (1538). To emphasise its prestige, the speakers nostalgically recall the courtly status that Catalan had formerly enjoyed, thus opposing the linguistically unitary vision of Spain put out by Marineo in his *De rebus Hispaniae memorabilibus opus* (1530). Livio decries the contrast between the courtly prestige of Catalan in the past and the growing Castilianisation of the Catalan nobility, identifying language with country and stating that, if Catalan disappeared, "that would make it look as if we'd been conquered by the Castilians".

Reflections on ecclesiastical matters occupy a good part of the first Dialogue. The speakers do not dwell on spiritual questions, but on church politics, from macropolitics (the war between Philip II and Pope Paul IV) to micropolitics (the far from exemplary behaviour of the bishop of Tortosa, Ferran de Loaces). In respect of both issues, Livio, the most daring of the speakers, puts his finger on the contradiction between the spiritual and the temporal powers of pope and bishop, and asserts that the pontiff should not own worldly possessions, whilst the other two speakers express their reservations.

On occasion these views have been linked to Erasmianism, but it would seem to be difficult to place the *Dialogues* strictly within that context. Such topics as outward religiosity, the pomp of divine office or the routine nature of the liturgy are not discussed in the work. What is more, in the controversy on knights and merchants, Livio and Don Pedro do not hesitate to defend, tooth and nail, the nobility's right to display its escutcheons on chapels and tombs. In fact, Erasmianism provides arguments for the defence of the monarchy or criticism of the bishop, but without the need to adopt core Erasmian values. Only surface elements are made use of, such as defending the royal jurisdiction not to respect the ecclesiastical immunity of the clergy, holding that "the Pope's arms ought to be spiritual, not made of steel", contrasting "a pastoral staff to lead and guard the flock" with "a sword and a lance to behead and disembowel", or maintaining a degree of scepticism when it comes to superstition and belief in miracles and relics.

Although expressed with force, the criticisms of the bishop of Tortosa — on the grounds that, despite the wealth he has at his disposal, he neither performs works of charity nor contributes to the building of the cathedral — in fact boil down to personal, rather than ideological, differences. The critique of the preferences and propensities of Pope Paul IV — based on his being a temporal as well as a spiritual lord, possesses immense wealth and puts his worldly interests before his spiritual ones — is primarily aimed at defending the interests of the Holy Roman Emperor and king of Spain, Charles V, in the war that brought him into conflict with the Pope over the control of Naples. Livio is upset by the fact that the pontiff's eagerness to acquire possessions should have made him go to war with Christian monarchs, and he hints that he had been aided and abetted by the Turks, the foulest enemies of the faith.

As for the Church's worldly goods and the temporal power of the Pope, Livio suggests that they ought to be self-regulated — that part of the tithes collected by the bishops should serve to finance the pontificate, but without having to maintain the Papal States. Faced with the astonishment of the other two speakers, he points to the Levites and to the military Order of St. John of Jerusalem as precedents. The question of the Church's wealth was highly topical, being intimately connected to the debate over the juridical and theological validity of the Donation of Constantine that was fanned in imperial circles with a view to putting an end to the power of the papacy, or at least weakening it. However, the *Dialogues* do not take up any of the legal or theological arguments in the debate, and they do not put forward any theories about the bases of the Pope's power, though the implied need for reform could well have come from Valdés' *Diálogo de las cosas acaecidas en Roma*.

The reflections on the municipal government of Tortosa — which take up almost the whole of the third Dialogue, whilst also appearing, though less often, in the first, fourth and sixth — are connected to questions regarding administrative ability and to the type of education that befits noblemen, patricians and merchants. Where the interests of knights and merchants met was in commerce, Catalan nobles believing it to be legitimate to increase their capital through business, which they even financed with loans from merchants. In the course of the dialogue the knight Don Pedro raises credits from merchants in Tortosa, so that the work's plot enacts the topic under discussion. Fabio, who belongs to the patriciate, argues in favour of the cultural function of trade, the defence of which does not, however, imply putting the two classes on the same level. Don Pedro and Livio make fun of the merchants' pretensions to have their trademarks regarded as equal to coats of arms and to having them carved on their mansions and their tombs.

The difference between the two, when it comes to education, is quite clear. Merchants should have a purely commercial training, whereas knights need to learn courtly accomplishments. The debate is sparked off by discussion of the patriciate. Whilst Fabio opts for what appears to have been the majority view in Tortosa, namely that their sons should be sent off to learn trades with the merchants of Barcelona or Valencia, Don Pedro and Livio reckon that they ought to be educated together with the sons of noble families. As for the syllabus, Livio holds up his own education as the correct model: "riding on every kind of saddle, jousting with all sorts of lances, fighting with all kinds of weapon, dancing every kind of dance, reading at set times all sorts of history books and, last but not least, always practising every sort of virtue." That, he argues, is how they can acquire qualities such as noble habits, greatness of spirit, courage, a sense of honour, and general knowledge. Surprisingly, though, going to university is not even suggested as an alternative to going to Court.

The cultural frontiers envisaged between knights and the patriciate are subtler, as both estates could share the same educational scheme and display the same good taste and courtesy in dress and behaviour. Livio goes so far as to suggest that the *ciutadans honrats*[3] ought to be listed in a register, like the nobility, as they were in Barcelona. On various occasions the speakers stress the improvement in manners in Tortosa: "Look how polished the citizens are, and how much better groomed, and how much more courteously they treat one another than they used to, and how much the ladies have improved in their deportment and their dress." These comments can readily be related to the model put forward by

---

3 J.H. Elliott defines *ciutadà honrat* – which in the present translation has generally been rendered by "patrician" – as follows: "A distinguished citizen of Barcelona or of some other town. The highest civic rank, hereditary by nature, and originally conferred either by royal grant or by election by the existing group of distinguished citizens, theoretically in recompense for services rendered to the city" *(The Revolt of the Catalans. A Study in the Decline of Spain (1598-1640)* [Cambridge, 1963], p. 573).

Castiglione in *Il Cortegiano*, as several passages in the *Dialogues* implicitly refer to that work, the differences lying in the fact that the Tortosa patriciate held the exclusive monopoly on the government of the city, to the nobility's detriment. In Livio's opinion, excluding the knights does not encourage the patricians' aspirations to a higher social status and puts the brakes on urban improvement, as they seek short-term profits and do not undertake large-scale reforms. On this point his argument with Fabio takes on a distinctly bitter tone, with Fabio's pride in the position that his class has attained clashing with Livio's Renaissance ambition to take part in public affairs in order to enhance the prosperity of the city.

Fabio actually shows off some of the urban improvements already achieved, like the bridge head of the Bridge of Boats, or that are still being built, such as the Renaissance fabric of the Royal Colleges, the most typically Renaissance building in Tortosa, and also the building going on in the cathedral. Livio, for his part, talks about the new projects that the town council ought to be promoting but is incapable of executing. In the last Dialogue the account of the resources in the lands bordering the Ebro — with its detailed catalogue of fish, birds, game and plants, compiled as the speakers sail and angle on the river — includes sharp criticism of the lack of initiatives aimed at developing those resources and making a profit out of them: the failure to encourage horse breeding or to exploit the mines, to build a foundry or to complete the irrigation scheme, despite the money that has already been invested in it. The defence of municipal government shared between knights and patricians, all of them educated by private tutors, is not based on the privileges acquired by them, for in fact those privileges excluded the knights, but on the practical benefits to be derived by the community.

Despuig's training and the way he sets out his ideas in the *Dialogues* are not those of a humanist, but his interests and concerns are those of a Renaissance writer. Although he often shows off his Classical references, the passages he selects, the way he refers to them and the lessons he draws from them are not typically humanistic, and in any case he mixes medieval references into them, although without creating conflicts of method. Instead, the modernity of his text and its Renaissance flavour derive from the fact that his analysis of reality is not grounded in divine providence, that he believes in the almost limitless possibilities of human beings to improve society, and that the speakers in his elegant controversy formulate divers opinions and make use of rhetorical argumentation in order to persuade each other that they are right. These elements are brought together by a set of critical reflections on contemporary life, by means of typically Renaissance multiple perspectives and by the development of an extraordinarily dynamic urban plot that pulls together the varied subjects that he treats. For all these reasons, Despuig's *Dialogues* should be regarded as a splendid example of the impact of the Renaissance on Catalan literature.

Enric Querol and Josep Solervicens

Translator's Preface

THE BASIC QUESTION for the translator of an Early Modern work must be whether or not to modernise it. I have not the slightest doubt that it would make little sense to present Cristòfol Despuig's *Dialogues* as a mock Tudor text. It is hard enough for a modern reader to grapple with a 450-year-old work translated out of a different language and culture, without having to do so through the fog of deliberately archaising English. What is more, the original was written in the language of its time for readers of its time. If, therefore, one wishes the translation to aspire to the kind of effect that the work had on its intended readers, one simply has no choice but to modernise.

But what kind of modern English should one aim for? Despuig locates his three speakers in everyday street scenes and interiors and, in the last Dialogue, has them sail and fish on the river Ebro, but his speakers do not just chat about everyday matters. They are educated, literate men, and — whilst they converse informally, often in jocular terms — they address a broad range of questions that exercise each others' intellects. Even though many of those questions are once again (or still) remarkably topical — most notably, Spanish attitudes towards Catalonia and the Catalan language — in the *Dialogues* they are discussed in the terms of their time. It would therefore be bizarre to present the speakers as if they were conspicuously living in the second decade of the twenty-first century. The challenge, as I see it, has been to attempt to produce an unostentatiously contemporary idiom — colloquial, but not slangy — that would read as convincingly as possible and do justice to those formulae typical of spontaneous conversation that the work's latest editors remark upon, such as colloquialisms, popular sayings, exclamations, oral syntax, redundancies and ellipses.

It will be as well for readers who are unfamiliar with Tortosa to be aware, from the start, that that city — roughly half-way between Barcelona and Valencia — lies just above the delta of the river Ebro, within the principality of Catalonia, whose capital was and still is Barcelona; that Catalonia was the driving force within the Crown of Aragon; and that in 1475 Aragon had been joined administratively to the Crown of Castile by the so-called Catholic monarchs, Ferdinand of Aragon and Isabella of Castile. It may also be helpful to note that Despuig uses the term Spain to denote the entire Iberian Peninsula, including Portugal.

Both in the text and in the introduction, I have anglicised place names, and also the names of monarchs and writers, when English versions of these exist — e.g. Castile (not Castilla), the Escorial (not El Escorial), John II (not Joan II) and Machiavelli (not Maquiavel). In the case of French monarchs, I have put them in French — François I (not Francisco), Henri II (not Enric).

The three speakers in Despuig's *Dialogues* often use the term "Senyor" ("Sir," "My dear Sir") when addressing one another, or attach that appellation to each others' names ("Senyor Fàbio", "Senyor Lívio", "Senyor Don Pedro"). I have omitted those forms of address, which jar with the object of presenting the work in, as far as possible, a modern idiom. In the latter cases I have left the proper names on their own ("Fabio", "Livio", "Don Pedro").

My only serious deliberate act of mistranslation concerns the title of the work, which Despuig gives, at the beginning of the dedication he penned to the count of Aitona, as *Los col·loquis de la insigne ciutat de Tortosa*. That can be rendered fairly literally as: *The Colloquies of the Notable City of Tortosa*. However, it has seemed sensible to highlight, by the word *Dialogues,* the important Renaissance genre to which the work belongs and to turn Despuig's title into a subtitle that defines the work as a Catalan Renaissance colloquy and indicates that the location of its action is Tortosa, but avoids implying that its subject matter is confined to that city, as the original title might suggest. Hence: Cristòfol Despuig, *Dialogues. A Catalan Renaissance Colloquy Set in the City of Tortosa*.

I have several thanks to express. First, to Josep Solervicens and to Joan Santanach for inviting me to attempt this translation and thus enabling me to discover and to relish what is undoubtedly a masterpiece

— a spirited promotion and critical defence of the reputation of the city
and district of Tortosa, and of Catalonia at large, which is saved from
going over the top by the gentle scepticism of the visitor to the city, Don
Pedro, and by what I take to be the witty exaggerations in the character
of the two Tortosans: Livio's almost excessive capacity for weaving historical arguments, and Fabio's conviction that just about everything in
Tortosa and its environs is the very best of its kind to be found anywhere
in the whole wide world. At the end of the fifth Dialogue, Livio himself
confesses to his listeners that he has been too long-winded and says he
fears he may have been boring them; and, in the last Dialogue, Don
Pedro refers to Fabio's catalogue of the amazing number of different
types of fishing tackle used in Tortosa as "quite a litany", a mildly
reproachful term that Fabio himself takes up immediately afterwards
when he introduces as "another litany" his impressive catalogue of water
fowl to be found in the Tortosa area, just one amongst his several lists of
local fauna and flora.

Speaking of which, I would have been up a gum tree if it hadn't been
for the appendix to Eulàlia Duran's edition of the work, in which she
offers Latin equivalents for nearly all the names of fish, shellfish,
quadrupeds, birds, plants, trees and mushrooms that Fabio enumerates.
None the less, on a very few occasions — when neither she nor other
means have enabled me to solve the problem — I have simply kept the
original Catalan term. I confess, however, to having had recourse to sub-
terfuge when it came to translating the list of words that Fabio reels off
relating to fishing tackle. The terms I have chosen cannot claim to be
exact equivalents of Fabio's, not least because many of the Catalan
names he uses (like a few of those for fauna and flora) do not appear anywhere other than in this work. Not only is it impossible to know what the
equivalent terms were in English — assuming that equivalent nets and
traps were known in England — but no-one even knows what exactly
most of them meant to Tortosans.

I have been fortunate enough to obtain indispensable expert assis-
tance with four further lexical problem areas. First, Despuig's *Dialogues*
use quite a few terms for social groups and for governmental, civic and
judicial institutions and officers, the problem here being that several of
them do not have precise equivalents in English. It is a pleasure to
acknowledge the help in this respect provided by such an undisputed
expert as James Amelang. Secondly, in translating the coats of arms of the
Despuig family and the city of Tortosa, it is through my good friend and

former colleague at the University of Southampton, Colin Platt, that Stephen Friar has kindly helped me out with the appropriate English heraldic jargon. Thirdly, another good friend and old colleague, Brian Sparkes, has provided translations of most of Despuig's Latin quotations, though I have left untranslated most of those whose meaning is made clear by the context. And, fourthly, in rendering the two laudatory Latin poems addressed to Despuig that he appends to his dedication of the work to the count of Aitona, I have worked from the translations of those poems into Catalan, made by Maria Paredes, that are included in the latest critical edition of the work: *Los col·loquis de la insigne ciutat de Tortosa* (Barcelona, Publicacions de l'Abadia de Montserrat, 2011).

This translation of the *Dialogues* — the first to be published in any language — is based on that edition and is preceded by a translation of the excellent scholarly introduction written for it by its editors, Enric Querol and Josep Solervicens, minus only its final sections on the transmission and reception of the text and on the textual criteria adopted by the editors.

Above all, it is a huge pleasure to acknowledge my debt of gratitude to Querol and Solervicens for their non-stop succour and support over several months. With unstinting generosity, they addressed my many queries, keeping up an instructive and stimulating correspondence that eerily echoed the dialogues of Don Pedro, Livio and Fabio — with me aping the role of the naïve and uninformed visitor, and they those of the two expert authorities. Without their help, on many occasions I should have been at a loss to fathom Despuig's meaning, or would simply have got it wrong.

The footnotes, which are deliberately minimal, are intended not to get in the way of what I hope will be an enjoyable read. They do not, therefore, attempt to clarify every last historical, geographical, bibliographical or lexicographical datum, but are there simply to provide the most basic information and to elucidate references that might otherwise puzzle the Anglophone reader. Most of them are based on those in the Querol-Solervicens edition, which is far more fully annotated.

Lastly, it goes very nearly without saying that the responsibility for the entire product is mine alone.[1]

Henry Ettinghausen
La Pera, March 2012

[1] This translation has been undertaken as part of the project "HUM-2005-02482-FILO" of the Secretaría General de Política Científica y Tecnológica of the Spanish Dirección General de Investigación.

DIALOGUES

The Colloquies of the Notable City of Tortosa, written by Mossèn[1]
Cristòfol Despuig, knight, in which are related the founding, the
antiquity, the name, the conquest, the freedom and the privileges of
the city, as well as the excellent, strange and marvellous things that
are to be found within its bounds, and also the diversity of the fruits
that are harvested there. In addition to salutary advice and counsels
for the good government and administration of the city and its
residents. Touching also upon various memorable and pleasant
stories, many of which are in praise of the Crown of Aragon
and, in particular, the Catalan nation. Dedicated to
the most illustrious lord, the count
of Aitona, in the year 1557.

---

[1] *Mossèn* was an honorific title used for priests and, as here, for secular worthies, most notably *ciutadans honrats.*

Dedication

LETTER OF DEDICATION of the present work to the most illustrious lord, the count of Aitona, high lord of the baronies of Xiva and Beniarjó, and chamberlain to the king, our lord.

MOST ILLUSTRIOUS LORD, according to the teachings of the excellent poet Horace in his *Art of Poetry*, no man should attempt a work to which his powers are not equal. Horace's actual words are these: "*Sumite materiam vestris, qui scribitis, aequam viribus.*" According to that teaching, I ought not to have set my hand to write what appears in these six Dialogues because, as regards the work itself, the difficulties were great, as may be gauged from its discourse; and, as regards myself, my ability is small. However, it seemed to me that to fail to apply myself might mean failing to make known what is fitting in respect of the honour and reputation of this city of Tortosa that has been so sadly forgotten in our times. Moreover, being as it is the city of my birth, and as I believe I owe particular attention to the memory of its ancient foundation, its true name, its history and the excellent and marvellous things that are to be found within its bounds, I have determined to undertake such a reasonable and justifiable enterprise in the belief that it would be more inappropriate to keep silent than to speak out, however imperfectly. For it is astonishing to find within the boundaries of one single city so many things that are rarely to be found within a whole kingdom, and few are the kingdoms in which so many can be found.

Thus, seeking to turn my weakness into strength, and confident that a bold spirit may overcome obstacles, I have determined to publish everything pertaining to this honourable and (to use Pliny's expression) *celebrated* city — for that is what he calls it — that I have seen with my own eyes and studied, written by divers authors and engraved in metal and stone. To be sure, the style is low and humble, but it is not inappropriate to the composition of dialogues. However, I assure your lordship that, as regards the truth, so far as has proved possible I have sought to follow what the most trustworthy authors have considered to be most certain.

Furthermore, even though the subject upon which I have decided to take up the pen is Tortosa, my principal purpose and intention has been to write about Catalonia — which is why the work intertwines other stories, most of which redound to the honour and the glory of the Crown of Aragon and, most particularly, the Catalan nation — both in order to embellish the work and to increase the pleasure of those who read it. It also offers some salutary advice and counsel for the government and good order of the city. And because Tortosa, amongst the other towns of Catalonia, came down on the side of making war on King John II of Aragon, following the arrest and death of Prince Charles of Viana, his son, I have decided to devote the whole of the fifth Dialogue to the causes of that war. I have done so with a view to explaining the cause that the king gave the Catalans to do what they did, and also in order to reply to what Lucio Marineo and others have written with greater attention to flattery than to the truth. I am aware that it might seem preferable to avoid speaking about anything to do with those troubles, in order to spare the memory of old sores and the irreparable harm they caused. However, since malevolent writers have not thought twice about recounting shameful slurs upon the Catalan nation, and seeing that what they have written is allowed to be published everywhere, I have regarded it as not only not bad, but actually very good and necessary, that I pen a defence, which may well be a good one, and it has seemed to me that it would have been a grave error to fail to write it.

I have not wished to write it in Castilian, both in order not to appear to slight the Catalan language and also so as not to use a foreign language to illustrate and defend what is our own identity, that being the principal intention of my work. Nor have I wished to write it in Latin, in order to prevent its being understood only by a small readership and by fewer amongst our nation than I would wish, as it is in their honour and for their pleasure that I have written it. None the less, it contains quotations from several weighty Latin authors which I have left in the original in order to avoid their losing the finesse and the distinction which that rich language confers. Even though those who do not know Latin will not understand them, that will not be an impediment to understanding the work in every other respect.

I have decided to dedicate the work to your lordship in the belief that that would be agreeable to you for two principal reasons: first, because Mossén Guillem Ramon de Montcada, your forebear, took the chief part in the conquest of Tortosa; secondly, because that same Montcada and his descendents were lords of Tortosa up to the time of King James II. And since, when speaking of Tortosa, it will inevitably be necessary speak of and recall the valour and the glory of the name of the Montcadas, whose head your lordship is throughout the whole of the Crown of Aragon, I may reasonably expect, as I say, that this service will be pleasing to you.

I beseech your lordship to be pleased to receive this service with the devotion with which it is offered, so that, with your lordship's favour and support, this work may be safeguarded against malicious tongues. And do not regard the work as small, even though it be so, for it cannot be said that he gives little who gives all he can, considering moreover that I am the first to dare undertake so arduous and difficult an enterprise, for it is certain that he does more who commences something than he who later only adds to it, "*quia facile est inventis addere*". May your lordship and others who read this work treat its shortcomings with patience and indulgence to match the good will with which it has been composed. And may Our Lord, as He can, protect the most illustrious person of your lordship with increase of states.

In Tortosa, etc.

EPIGRAM TO THE NOBILITY AND TO
THE RENOWNED VIRTUES OF CRISTÒFOL DESPUIG,
BY JAUME VIDAL[2]

Muse, I sing, in Latin verse, famous deeds
and a man renowned for his ancient rank.
Clio of Cythera, Queen of Pieria, first daughter
of the Supreme Father and honour of Jupiter,
you celebrate the deeds of great men,
the prizes worthy of triumphant hands,
the crowns of Mars' heroes, even lusty wars
and all that has been famed throughout the world.
Thus, then, slipping through the breezes, come inspire
in my mind a glorious song, now that I commence these lines.
Well disposed, wet from sacred waters,
with your golden locks encircling your placid temples,
from the ship from Meonia you will recite sweet chants,
and the learned lyres will give out the music of Pegasus.
Coupled to these measures, they have made gentle verses
that have made the well-stretched strings resound.
I thus desire that your fitting hand may temper
the noted praise that I shall speak with exalted melodies.
What do we not all owe to generous Despuig?
What an illustrious and magnanimous man for us all!
With a heart like Hector's, he outshines the ancient heroes:
Alcidas, whose deeds are seen throughout the ages,
except in ours; Achilles, never vanquished, were he still alive,
and had not been carried off by the Fates;
Laertes' son, leader of the Achaian squadrons,
mighty in strength and intrepid; and ferocious Camillus
who overcame his foes with admirable cunning.
If, finally, the sturdy heart of noble Quintus Fabius
may bear the routed arms from Rome,
do you think, oh Muse, that anyone would wish
to deny my Despuig that prize?

[2] Jaume Vidal (Tortosa, c. 1510/15-1586) belonged to Despuig's social circle and had received his support in 1547 when he applied for a benefice.

The glory of a famous lineage illuminates Despuig,
and the celebrated paternal emblems of a magnificent house,
bequeathed by distinguished parents of noble stock,
as is proven by a prized medallion engraved in gold.
He himself brings the rewards of his exalted virtue
which will surely be remembered with perpetual honour.
Whatever they say about the thoughts of Cato,
the venerable feats hidden by the old muse of Samos
and the rituals celebrated by the ancients,
be they the famous Delphic oracles or what the works of Greeks
[dictate,
we can learn from you with living instances
those Roman deeds that you tell in your works.
You, captain, helmsman, glory of our land,
you have prizes worthy of everlasting honour.
You possess, first, the insignia of the order of knights,
and the highest civil laurels are yours, too.[3]
And, after these achievements, to say the truth
and speak openly and properly of the facts,
whether by unanimous decision or by a learned and solemn assembly,
the favourable opinion of either bears more weight than yours,
as your feelings come from a mighty heart.
The alarms of war resound, and if at any time, with awful weapons,
the enemy's generals have reached the high walls,
you advance with Caesarian valour and drag the solid cohorts
and the merciless troops to interminable struggles.
Your right hand will bring together
the cavalry squadrons separated by the rapid march,
and in this place these famous feats will be remembered from now on.
Why do I explain in my verses deeds that should be watched over in
[vigil
that must surely serve to enhance the glory of a greater poet?
Despite all, the pallid Muse is favourable to me.
Thus, then, as patron, receive my poems,
however simple they may sound,
for being born far from the nobility does not prevent
the composition of lofty songs. They please the mind,

3 Despuig was, in fact, a *donzell* or squire — not a knight — and was thus able to take an active part in the governance of Tortosa, which was not open to the higher nobility.

they are fitting for undertakings told by serene souls,
though they be written by such a humble hand.
Still this remains: that when the years have passed
and the Fates allow me, as I wish, to live with you,
I may transmit what only celestial spirits can inspire,
making vain promises come true.
If God does thus, beginning with good fortune,
my verses will arrive at a good port.
Your writings will forever make your deeds
fly amongst men from mouth to mouth.
They will see your magnanimity, your high-born blood,
the great glory that you lend your ancestors.
Another time I shall speak of the future,
which will have to be told with greater skill.
Meanwhile, fare well! I tell of generous and renowned feats,
and I shall always be a follower of your house.

PERE CERDÀ,[4] DOCTOR IN CIVIL AND CANON LAW, TO
CRISTÒFOL DESPUIG, URGING HIM TO PUBLISH HIS *DIALOGUES*

The people, patricians, knights, our whole republic,
beg you to publish, as does the work itself.
Tarry no longer, Despuig! Generously act!
The French praise your name,
and happy Catalonia celebrates your divine fame.
Come, all Aragon makes pious pleas,
benign Valencia beseeches you with humble supplication.
The moistened sponge has polished your brilliant book.
Fabius' hesitation benefited ancient Rome,
and this delay will profit the Spaniards.
Whoever desires to know the origins of the Hesperian people
need go no further. Despuig, you explain it with supreme art.
I say this man from Tortosa explains
ancient, forgotten, tales in admirable order.
He has shown that the broad waters of past deeds flow
and can gently avoid the reefs in the sea.
His pure language has disentangled the hidden deeds of the
                                                    [ancients,
the grave obstacles and the powerful arms of the leaders.
But, worthier of your counsel and your exalted mind,
Tortosa prevails, with you as protector, and honours you.
When you speak, when you gloss the feats of men and kings,
the fountain of Castalia flows from your smooth lips.
Tortosa, land of your fathers, will thank you for this hard task
and will grant you prizes worthy of your worth.
You restore them, as did great Camillus!
Live, then, captain, as long as Nestor!

4 Pere Cerdà (Tortosa, c. 1514-1592) was a distant relation of Despuig.

The First Dialogue

THE FIRST DIALOGUE OF THE CITY OF TORTOSA. IN WHICH, ON THEIR WAY TO ATTEND MASS, A KNIGHT AND A GENTLEMAN, BORN AND BRED IN THAT CITY, MEET A KNIGHT WHO HAS JUST ARRIVED FROM VALENCIA, AND IN WHICH THE THREE OF THEM DISCUSS VARIOUS TOPICS TOUCHING UPON TORTOSA, ITS CATHEDRAL AND OTHER MATTERS.

Speakers:
FABIO, a gentleman; LIVIO, a knight;
DON PEDRO, a knight from Valencia.

FABIO: The sun's up, and you're still at home! Livio, it's high time we went to mass!

LIVIO: You've beaten me to it! I was just about to go to your house to say the same thing! Let's be off right away to do our spiritual duty. Then we'll be able to employ ourselves better in temporal matters.

FABIO: That's an excellent idea! That way we'll kill two birds with one stone!

LIVIO: Fabio, if my eyes don't deceive me, that knight over there talking to that merchant is our friend Don Pedro! But why should he have taken it into his head not to come straight to my house? After all, he knows perfectly well that he's always welcome. Yes, it really *is* him! And it looks as if he's laughing at seeing me looking so surprised. He's coming over here!

FABIO: There's no doubt about it. It's him, for sure! I could tell by the way he holds himself and by his lively demeanour that he was a Valencian, but I didn't realise it was Don Pedro.

LIVIO: How come, Don Pedro, that you're in Tortosa and not at my house? I can hardly believe what I'm seeing!

DON PEDRO: Well, doubting Thomas believed, once he'd seen! Don't tell me you're a harder nut to crack than he was!

LIVIO: I wonder if you're capable of doing what those people did, once upon a time, in your city of Valencia at Mossèn Marrades' house![5]

DON PEDRO: They weren't people. They were devils!

FABIO: People say that what they did was grotesque and monstrous.

DON PEDRO: It was so monstrous that I don't wish to talk about it.

LIVIO: Let's forget it, then, for now. Just tell us why on earth you didn't come straight to my house!

DON PEDRO: It's just that I got here so late last night that the gate at the end of the bridge was already shut.

FABIO: The main gate was, but not the postern. They never lock that. The area on the other side of the bridge is being built up to such an extent that the postern has to be kept open in case there's an emergency.

LIVIO: But the hostelries over on the other side are there just to meet needs such as Don Pedro had last night.

DON PEDRO: You're perfectly right. And they're also useful for people who don't wish to be observed, though that wasn't my case. Whenever I come here I enter the city and just enjoy walking about. To my way of thinking, it's the most peaceable one in the world. And it looks as though we enjoy it all the more because it's the first city that we come across in our ancient native land.

FABIO: What do you mean by your ancient native land?

DON PEDRO: What I mean is that we Valencians came from Catalonia, and we regard those families that didn't come from Catalonia as inferior. And we use the language of Catalonia, even though it's been badly affected by the fact that we're so close to Castile.

FABIO: But don't you say Valencia was conquered by King James of Aragon?[6] Didn't the Aragonese play a part in regaining the city from the Moors?

DON PEDRO: Yes, but the troops and the main forces involved were all, or nearly all, Catalan. That's why the language that's spoken there is Catalan, not Aragonese. Which isn't to say that no Aragonese noblemen or other families settled there and, indeed, remain there to this day.

---

5 The reference is to some ghostly apparitions in Valencia in 1542.
6 James I of Aragon, known as 'the Conqueror' (1208-1276).

FABIO: Pere Antoni Beuter gives a different explanation for the survival of Catalan in Valencia. He says the Catalan language took root there because a number of young women from Lleida were taken there to help populate the city, and children learn more from their mothers than from their fathers.

DON PEDRO: Yes, I know Pere Antoni says that, but his opinion isn't very convincing if you reckon that those ladies only populated the city of Valencia, whereas Catalan spread throughout the entire kingdom, and it's still spoken all the way from Orihuela to Traiguera. What he says doesn't square with what I say, which is that at that time the king didn't just *speak* Catalan, but used it in all his writings. That's why Catalan took root there, and not Aragonese.

LIVIO: There's no two ways about it. And the same goes for Majorca, which was also conquered by King James, as well as Menorca and Ibiza when they were conquered. That's why Catalan came to be spoken on all those islands, and still is, just as it was at the beginning. They had no need to change it, as they did in Valencia or in Sardinia, which was conquered by Prince Alfonso, who later became king of Aragon.[7] The Sardinians also have the Catalan language, even though not all of them speak it, as the ancient language of that kingdom still survives in many parts of the island. However, the knights and people of a certain social standing, as well as those engaged in business, speak Catalan, because there Catalan is the language of prestige.

DON PEDRO: Actually, I don't see why. After all, Catalan isn't held in such great esteem. In fact, Aragonese is thought to be superior, because it's closer to Castilian.

LIVIO: That's true today, but in the olden days Aragonese was regarded as extremely unrefined, as indeed it was, which is why it was held to be inferior to our language. That's shown by the fact that the kings — even though they called themselves kings of Aragon — didn't speak Aragonese, but Catalan. Even King Martin, the last in the male line of the counts of Barcelona, spoke Catalan. And his father, Peter III, wrote the chronicle of the feats of his grandfather and his father, as well as his own, in the Catalan language, as you can see to this day in the manuscript that he penned with his own hand

---

7 Alfonso III of Catalonia-Aragon, known as 'the Benign', conquered Sardinia in 1324, before he came to the throne.

that's kept in the royal archives in Barcelona and which Pere Miquel Carbonell has included in his chronicle of Catalonia. In a moment I'll tell you something else that backs up my argument and which is worth thinking about — the fact that in Aragon, which borders on Catalonia and Valencia, those who live even two or three leagues from the border haven't got a notion of the Aragonese language. That's a fact, just as I'm telling it to you. Which is why I get so annoyed when I see how nowadays Castilian is being embraced by the principal noblemen and knights of Catalonia, even in Barcelona, especially seeing how in former times the magnanimous kings of Aragon refused to countenance such an abuse. I'm not saying Castilian isn't a perfectly proper language, and recognized as such. And I admit that all important people need to know it, because Spanish is the language that's known throughout Europe. But I do condemn and denounce its everyday use amongst ourselves, because that could lead to our language being gradually uprooted from our land, and that would make it look as if we'd been conquered by the Castilians.

DON PEDRO: I don't disagree with what you say. There's no doubt that that abuse is being taken at least as far in Valencia as it is here, if not further. I wish everyone would give some thought to the issue.

FABIO: I reckon there isn't much that can be done about it. Which is why I think it's pointless to worry about it, Don Pedro, and even more pointless after what we've already said. In any case, I'm very pleased that our language has prevailed over Aragonese in the kingdom of Valencia and on those islands. But let's change the subject! Don Pedro, why is the merchant you were talking to just now still waiting over there? Go and say goodbye to him, and let's go to mass.

DON PEDRO: He isn't waiting for me. I've finished the business I was doing with him. All I wanted from him was a loan of a hundred ducats, plus credit of five hundred for the days I'm going to be in Barcelona.

LIVIO: What a shame it is that we knights have such great needs that we have to rely on people like that all the time!

FABIO: But surely they're of benefit to the world. Apart from the services they provide for their own gain, thanks to their business dealings a lot of news reaches people from all over the world which wouldn't do so otherwise.

DON PEDRO: There's no doubt about that. In fact, trade is an art that's been held in high esteem for a long time now, and practiced by plenty of knights and gentlemen, as indeed it still is in Valencia.

LIVIO: The same's true of Barcelona and of other places. I've been told that here in Tortosa, too, trade used to be well looked upon.

FABIO: I can vouch for that as well as anyone. I've got books at home, and I've seen others in other people's houses, that show that once upon a time trade boomed here and was practiced far and wide.

DON PEDRO: That would have been as far away as Barcelona and Valencia.

FABIO: That's a good one! Why not say as far away as Genoa, Rome, Naples, Venice, Cyprus and Sicily; and, in the west, as far as Cadiz, Seville and Portugal, and even Flanders and England, and beyond?

LIVIO: Holy Mary! Do you really mean that trade spread as far as that? If that's the case, I'm not surprised that most gentlemen's houses have their trademarks carved in stone and that they hold them in as great esteem as their coats of arms.

DON PEDRO: And they do well to do so. Since nowadays they haven't got as much money as when they were engaged in trade, at least they've still got those marks for the next time they have enough money to start up a business again.

LIVIO: It would be just as good to have money as trademarks. But, as far as keeping their trademarks is concerned, I can assure you that that's what they do. Yes, indeed! And I'll have you know that they even have them put on their chapels and their tombs.

DON PEDRO: I don't believe it!

LIVIO: It's a fact!

FABIO: Livio, don't you think their trademarks ought to be there?

LIVIO: No, I don't!

FABIO: Nor their coats of arms?

LIVIO: Yes, their coats of arms are all right.

FABIO: How's that? Aren't they both worldly emblems? Why should one of them be there, and not the other? The way I see it, there's more reason to have their trademarks there than coats of arms, because in a way they imply peace, whereas arms refer to war. Surely, in a church it's better to have symbols of peace than of war?

LIVIO: The way you've coloured your argument, it looks as if there's no way anyone could disagree with you. But, in actual fact, you're completely mistaken. The truth is the exact opposite of what you think. Even though both kinds of sign are worldly, which I readily admit, and even though, as such, they aren't worthy of being allowed in holy places, arms are symbols of the art of war, and armies are there chiefly in order to fight and wipe out enemies in just wars. Enemies against whom war is just are those who are opposed to the Church — like the Turk, the Moor, the heathen, the heretic or the schismatic. It follows, then, that the instrument whereby justifiable enemies are opposed must be regarded as just. In which case, it's just and reasonable that it be allowed in the house of the just, which is the church, as defender of the Church. None of these considerations apply to trademarks, whereas they do to flags and other military insignia, which are allowed specifically and rightly in Catalonia, because those who placed them there fought gloriously with them.

FABIO: I've had enough of arguing with you. You're too good at sophistry!

DON PEDRO: Tell me then, for heaven's sake, why do you put those symbols there? Do you want them to be able to enjoy ecclesiastical immunity?

LIVIO: I would say so.

DON PEDRO: Well, I don't know if they will be all that safe there. Nowadays things to do with the Church aren't respected as much as they used to be.

FABIO: How do you mean?

DON PEDRO: Don't you see how priests are treated nowadays, at least in Valencia? They're defrocked for absolutely no reason at all. And if that can't be done, they're removed from the jurisdiction of the bishops by maliciously applying a papal brief. And, even if the brief is issued in order to carry out a sentence, they only use it to exact extortion and injustice.[8]

LIVIO: That brief also applies here in Catalonia. But what you're saying springs from the malice and hatred that some people have towards the Church. Even if things were the way you describe them, it's all our fault, and we deserve it for not being satisfied and obeying our king, let alone God. God allows it so that, in His name and under the protection of the Church, we don't lose our souls, as well as our bodies.

DON PEDRO: You *are* a pious man, Livio! What is all this? Do you want to rule the world? Are you aiming for some royal appointment or other?

LIVIO: I'm not that ambitious, but I can't help speaking the truth. I'd do so for a Moor, otherwise the Crown would look like an instrument for evil, rather than for combating evil.

[8] The papal brief referred to was issued by Julius III in 1553.

FABIO: Well, I've heard you speak differently on other occasions.

LIVIO: That would have been when I was moved by passion. As the excellent Catalan philosopher and poet Ausiàs March says, passion clouds the mind.[9]

FABIO: Ah, but we know very well where all the harm comes from, and it isn't from where you think, Livio. Priests are no worse now than they used to be. Let's not try to gild tin. Let's just speak the truth.

LIVIO: Where does the harm come from, then?

FABIO: From the fact that ministers and officials applaud the king, not because they want to serve him but because, in their own interest, they go in for extortion and a thousand other abuses. They want to turn the king into a tyrant, even though he isn't one by nature.

DON PEDRO: We're just knocking our heads against a brick wall! No respect is shown to the Pope, even though he's the Prince of the Church, and you expect them to show respect for a mere priest!

FABIO: What do you mean, they don't respect the Pope?

DON PEDRO: Don't you see the open warfare that King Philip of Spain is waging against Pope Paul IV? If God doesn't do something about it, everything's going to go to blazes![10]

LIVIO: We certainly do see it, Don Pedro, but it's all the Pope's fault. He could easily avoid war. As I say, just as it's their fault that priests are oppressed, it's the Pope's fault if they make war on him.

DON PEDRO: Really? If that's the case, just explain why, and I'll be pleased to be enlightened.

LIVIO: Please don't ask me to get bogged down in an explanation. For heaven's sake, don't make me talk about the Pope. After all, he's forbidden us to talk about him. As he's my lord and master in spiritual matters, I don't wish to displease or disobey him.

DON PEDRO: You don't have to criticise his powers or talk about articles of faith. But when it comes to his wishes and intentions, and other lesser matters, it seems to me that you can talk about him without any scruples of conscience, especially if we just speak amongst ourselves and it doesn't go any further. And there's absolutely no need for us to be malicious.

---

9 The Valencian Ausiàs March (1397-1459), regarded as one of the greatest Catalan poets, was the first major poet to write entirely in Catalan.

10 Paul IV was Pope from 1554 to 1559. The reference here is to the invasion of the Papal States in 1556 — by the duke of Alba, in the name of Philip II of Spain — for the control of the kingdom of Naples.

LIVIO: I certainly shan't say anything that I don't think I've got a right to say, but I wouldn't say anything to do with the Pope except on the understanding that it's entirely between the three of us — as you say, it won't go any further. And I'll talk about things that are ruled by the senses when they dominate reason, just as much when talking about the Pope as about other men. After all, he's a man like the rest of us. As far as his person is concerned, you can't say anything that isn't favourable. From what we know about the beginning of his pontificate, and from what they say about his rectitude and his holiness, he's an exceptional prince. However, often it's the people who are close to princes who are responsible for making them lose their good nature, and it would seem that that's the case with the Pope. But if by any chance I'm wrong in what I understand people to be saying, just ignore what I say. In any case, I submit to the orders and the correction of the Holy Roman Church.

DON PEDRO: That's fine, and it's taken as read. But now, tell us why the Pope is to blame for the war.

LIVIO: Do you want an explanation in just a few words? It's because he wanted to take away the kingdom of Naples from King Philip, even though it's his by inheritance, and it's perfectly proper for the king to defend it. After all, natural law allows you to defend what's yours.

DON PEDRO: Yes, but the Pope claimed the kingdom *de jure*, by way of his attorney general, whereas the king claimed it *de facto*.

LIVIO: The Pope wanted to get hold of Naples *de jure* and *de facto*. And, in order to do so, he joined forces with the king of France, and with other princes and potentates of Christendom — and even, so they say, with the Grand Turk![11]

FABIO: With the Turk? That's impossible! At least, I can't believe it!

LIVIO: I wouldn't wish to believe it either, but that's what people say.

DON PEDRO: Let's forget about that, as it really is incredible. But didn't the king of France sign a truce with King Philip? If so, how come you say he's joined forces with the Pope against the king with whom he'd signed a truce?

LIVIO: He had indeed. But, he broke the truce to be able to back the Pope, so that, once war was declared, he could try to take control of the duchy of Milan and the kingdom of Naples, because he can't stomach the idea of those two states belonging to anyone else.

---

[11] Suleiman the Magnificent (1494-1566), the longest reigning sultan of the Ottoman Empire.

DON PEDRO: What a mess! If only states like that just didn't exist! That way, Christendom wouldn't be breaking up, as it's in danger of doing. The Turk could well say that both those kings are doing more for him than half of his own empire! If it weren't for them, he wouldn't be living safe and sound in his palace, and he wouldn't be triumphing over Christendom, as he's been doing up to now, taking the impregnable island of Rhodes, as well as Buda, Belgrade and nearly the whole of Hungary, and, more recently, Béjaïa in Barbary.[12] Now he's threatening what little is left of the Christian possessions in Africa. This entire disaster would come to a stop if only the strife and conflict over those two execrable states came to an end. Even though there are other bones of contention between the kings of France and Spain, such as the duchy of Burgundy, as well as other more minor quarrels over Flanders, it's the squabbles over Italy that really get in the way and can't be resolved. If only part of that problem could be sorted out, the rest would virtually fade away. And, once that happened, there's no question that they'd join forces and, together, bring the Turk to his knees.

FABIO: Do either of you know what rights the king of France thinks he's got in Italy?

LIVIO: I know what rights he thinks he's got in Italy, and in Burgundy, too. But it would take a long time to explain.

FABIO: Well, let's forget about it, then, and get back to the war that's being fought between the Pope and the king of Spain. Even though I don't know as much about these things as you two, since I've still got a right to my opinion I'll let you know what I think. Tell me, Livio, because it's you I want to talk to, as you're the one who's blaming the Pope, don't you know that the kingdom of Naples belonged to the Church and that, due to the excessive generosity of one of the popes, it was assigned to a particular king, implying great prejudice to the Church?[13] So, if the present Pope sees that the damage done was so enormous and that that's the reason why the Church is impoverished, why shouldn't he take back what by right belongs to the Church in order to meet its needs?

LIVIO: Either the Pope had the right to establish his rule, or he didn't. If he did, there's no reason why he should take it back. And, if not, he shouldn't attempt to obtain it by means of scandalous violence.

---

[12] Rhodes came under Turkish domination in 1522, Buda in 1526, Belgrade in 1521, parts of Hungary in 1552, and Béjaïa in 1555.

[13] The reference is to the investiture of King Alfonso the Magnanimous in 1443.

FABIO: First of all, the king was warned that he was to return Naples according to law and custom. So, if he still refuses to renounce his control over the kingdom, why shouldn't the Pope do what he can?

LIVIO: No, actually it would be better if the Pope and the Church, in whose name he speaks, didn't obtain the kingdom, or indeed anything at all, getting hold of this and defending that with scandal and violence and in such adverse circumstances as now prevail — with the Turk at the gates threatening us in Italy, and the Lutherans occupying nearly the whole of Germany and France, and not knowing whether Greece has been lost. Just look what's become of England! The fact is that in Europe, which is just about the only place where Christ's name is honoured, Italy and Spain are almost the only countries that are still untainted. And, as far as Spain is concerned, just look at what's happened in Castile! If we didn't have such a very Catholic king and the benefit of the holy Inquisition, we wouldn't be safe in our own homes. That's why, if you press me hard, I'd say this is no time for the Pope to be asking what he's asking for. What's more, if he's in danger of losing what he's got, he shouldn't put up any resistance in order not to endanger the unity of the Christian princes in the face of the Turk, for they say he's about to descend on us in strength.

Besides, if the Pope had nothing to defend, he wouldn't feel like taking up arms against Christians. Just think! What could be more outrageous or unreasonable than the Pope — whose only purpose ought to be instructing us regarding the spiritual life and persuading us with words and examples to embrace humility and temperance — spending his time ruling temporal kingdoms and, in order to do so, having armies and all kinds of engines of war to kill men? In truth, Fabio, the Pope's arms ought to be spiritual, not made of steel! In any case, don't you know that the wisest doctors advise amputating a limb infected by Saint Anthony's fire, if that means saving the whole body, rather than avoiding amputation and putting the whole body at risk?[14] In which case, wouldn't it be better if the Pope lost, or didn't gain, the kingdom of Naples, which is the affected limb, rather than insist on joining it to the Church and losing the entire body, which is Christendom?

DON PEDRO: It looks, Livio, as if you don't agree with the Church having possessions?

---

[14] Saint Anthony's fire was one of the names for ergotism, or ergot poisoning.

LIVIO: No, I really don't.

DON PEDRO: Why not?

LIVIO: For a thousand reasons that I've read and heard, and even seen, regarding the whole business of Church possessions. They've been the cause of great scandals in Christendom, as was predicted by that voice from the heavens that was heard on the day Emperor Constantine gave up the Roman throne to the Church, as St. Vincent Ferrer recalls in a sermon for the sixth day after Pentecost when he speaks about those who waste church property.

DON PEDRO: And what did that voice say?

LIVIO: What St. Vincent Ferrer wrote is this: "When the Emperor Constantine gave revenues to the Church for God, there was heard, as is said by some, on the very same day, a voice in the heavens saying: 'Today in the Church of God poison has been planted'."[15] And that's been shown to be true an infinite number of times. Whenever a Pope has wished to keep hold of this, or get hold of that, he's always needed to hold in his hand not a pastoral staff to lead and guard the flock, but a sword and a lance to behead and disembowel.

DON PEDRO: So, you still insist that the Pope ought to have no possessions at all? How then could he live with the authority and the majesty that befit him? Would you want him to live with no other income than what dispatching papal bulls brings in, and so have to face even greater problems? Let him be as saintly and as sober as you wish, and indeed as I do too, but don't you want the greatest of all princes — the universal prince of the Church — to live like a prince? How is he to do that if you remove all his possessions?

LIVIO: I'll tell you how. Or at least I'll tell you how I think he could. Every year the Pope could be given part of the tithes and the first fruits that all the bishops and clergy of Christendom live off — enough so that, altogether, he could live like a Pope. That wouldn't just enable him to live with the majesty due to Christ's vicar. It would also be a healthy exercise in reducing the rents enjoyed by the prelates and the rest of the clergy, because the surplus fat that they've got doesn't do them any good. "All things in excess do harm", as King Solomon says.[16]

FABIO: What Livio says doesn't sound bad to me, but how could it be done?

---

[15] In the original, the quotation is in Latin.

[16] In the original: *"Quia omne nimium nocet."*

LIVIO: It would only take the Pope and all the princes in Christendom to want it, and the means would be found soon enough!

DON PEDRO: It's certainly a new idea! Nothing like that has ever been seen!

LIVIO: You're wrong about that. That's roughly the way the Levites lived amongst the people of Israel. Joshua didn't give them a portion of the Promised Land, because God told him not to. The other tribes had their portions shared out between them, and the portions were managed by the priests. Only the Levites were allowed to manage them. And that's also roughly the way in which the Order of St. John manages its affairs. It's so well off that each Grand Master gives a certain portion of the monies he's got to the treasury of the Order for its maintenance.

DON PEDRO: I don't disagree with what you're saying. In fact, I tend to go along with your argument. But, going back to the war that those two princes are waging, I say it's very unfortunate for King Philip, just as it was for the Emperor his father, that at the beginning of their reigns they've had the ill fortune to wage war against the vicar of Christ and the Church, seeing that they're such Catholic princes and such zealous defenders of Christianity.

LIVIO: That's perfectly true, but it's a great relief for them to know that it wasn't their fault. They were provoked into war. They had no other choice but to reply with war. As our Catalan saying has it: "Even if you don't want to, you can be forced to go to court or to take sides."

FABIO: What? Are you telling me that the Emperor, too, went to war with the Pope?

DON PEDRO: Well, didn't he? Of course, he did!

FABIO: Which Pope was that, then, and why did they go to war?

DON PEDRO: It was Clement VII.[17] And the reason was that selfsame kingdom of Naples. And he had François I, king of France, to support him, just as the present Pope has got the present French king, Henri II. And the league and the concordat that they agreed amongst themselves against the Emperor were such that, before they even declared war, they'd already shared out Naples between them!

FABIO: Holy Mary! So how did the whole affair turn out for the Emperor?

17 Clement VII was Pope from 1523 to 1534.

DON PEDRO: Very well indeed! He beat all his enemies, thanks to the force of the just claim that he had on his side. He made the king of France prisoner, and the Pope as well, and he took Rome and ended up beating France and becoming master of all Italy.[18]

FABIO: So couldn't the Pope have deduced from those events that God isn't pleased with his conduct?

DON PEDRO: As far as I can see, he must have thought about that, but I expect he's so tied up and controlled by his relatives that he just can't act any differently.

FABIO: Talking of his relatives, what makes them want to indulge in such an iniquitous undertaking?

DON PEDRO: The simple ambition to rule. It's so powerful that it makes men betray their principles and lose their sense of judgement. In the end, it turns them into rabid dogs.

FABIO: Didn't you say the Pope wants to win Naples back in order to give it back to the Church, to which he says it used to belong?

DON PEDRO: That may well be his intention, but it isn't what his relatives have in mind. Once the kingdom is back in the Pope's hands, they intend governing it. They want it for themselves, and that's what they've decided. They've already worked out who'll get what, the same as in Pope Clement's day.

FABIO: May Christ sort all this out! He's the only one who can! And now let's go to mass. It's about to start.

LIVIO: There's no need to worry about that. After all, from seven o'clock till eleven they say mass non-stop in St. Candia's chapel. First we can take a stroll in the cathedral so that Don Pedro can see the new building works that have been going on there.[19]

DON PEDRO: I'm told that pious St. Candia is venerated throughout all these lands.[20]

FABIO: She certainly is. And not just around here, but in nearly the whole of Spain. People from Castile and many other parts send for holy ribbons to seek cures from the glorious saint for all sorts of ills, especially scrofulous swellings on the neck. And they're quite right

---

[18] The reference is to the imperial victory at Pavia in 1525 and to the sack of Rome by Charles V's troops in 1527.

[19] The present catedral, begun in the 14th century, was not completed until the Baroque façade was built in the 18th century.

[20] The head of St. Candia, an ancient patroness of the city, had been venerated in one of the cathedral's chapels since the mid-14th century.

to do so, because they can see with their own eyes that God's always pleased to work great miracles through her intercession for the benefit of mankind, curing them of such nasty complaints.

DON PEDRO: That really is most remarkable! Give thanks to the Lord for the jewel that you have here. But, God bless me! What a marvellous job they're doing on the building! How mighty and pious it looks with all that alabaster!

FABIO: So you like it, do you?

DON PEDRO: I most certainly do. It's one of the most exquisitely built cathedrals I've ever seen. Once it's completed, it will be a veritable temple. To my way of thinking, these alabaster carvings are even better than the stained glass windows.

FABIO: At least the cathedral is better sheltered, and they can paint images of the saints as big as you can see them over there. They couldn't be painted so well on glass, because that's made up of little pieces.

DON PEDRO: What I say is that I find it all very much to my taste. Tell me, has the cathedral put a lot of its income aside for the works?

FABIO: No. In fact, very little.

DON PEDRO: So, how come they're building it so sumptuously?

FABIO: They're sharing the expenses somehow between the bishop and the clergy — and the city is helping out, too.

DON PEDRO: The city? Is the cathedral chapter so poor that it needs the city's help?

FABIO: Actually, the chapter isn't very well endowed, but there are plenty of donations.

DON PEDRO: How can the cathedral fail to be well off, seeing how well off its dignitaries are? Haven't you heard the saying that there's no such thing as a poor king in a rich kingdom?

FABIO: Yes, but that's when love and charity abound and when people prefer the public good to private profit. Here things are different, and custom soon becomes law.

DON PEDRO: So how many dignitaries and canonries are there in this cathedral?

FABIO: A dozen dignitaries and a score of canonries.

DON PEDRO: A dozen dignitaries?

FABIO: Yes, indeed, twelve. And they're all very well endowed. Even if they were reduced in order to help pay the Pope a little, as Livio was suggesting earlier, they'd still be extremely good.

DON PEDRO: What are they actually worth, then?

FABIO: They're worth different amounts. They aren't all the same. Some of them account for two thousand pounds, others for over a thousand, and some for eight hundred.

DON PEDRO: Jesus! Is that possible? That really is quite something! If you hadn't told me, I should never believe it. And where does the money come from to pay them?

FABIO: From very good tithes and first fruits, both within the city bounds and in the whole of the diocese. One of them, the chief priory, gets its main income from some very important mills.

DON PEDRO: I can tell you, they're one of the most beautiful things I've seen in this kingdom of Aragon. And what are the canonries worth?

FABIO: Actually, the canonries aren't very well endowed, and they depend on the dignitaries annexed to them. It was all badly conceived from the very beginning, when the church resources were divided up. That made for very poor canonries, which is a great misfortune. However, that isn't the worst of it, as experience shows us every day. Since the dignitaries are so well endowed, every day they're hunted for by powerful outsiders, so that, bit by bit, we'll end up losing them. Unless some of them can be recovered by local priests, we'll soon have lost them all. It's just the opposite with the canonries, and it would be, even if they were far better endowed, because they derived their income, and still do, from allowances and assignments that require personal attendance and service, which is something that outsiders wouldn't be so happy with.

DON PEDRO: So what *are* the canonries worth?

FABIO: A hundred and fifty pounds.

DON PEDRO: That isn't bad! The canons should be able to live quite decently, even on that, in a place like Tortosa, as I suppose life here must be quite cheap.

FABIO: Yes, it is. And they don't have many obligations or ceremonies to attend to, which makes life a lot easier.

DON PEDRO: And the bishopric? How much is that worth?

FABIO: It must be worth nine or ten thousand pounds.

DON PEDRO: You're joking!

FABIO: No, I'm not. That's how it is. And the diocese covers an enormous area. It's at least thirty Catalan leagues long, starting at a town called Maials, a couple of leagues from the river Segre, and reaching as far as Almenara, five leagues from Valencia. And it also extends into Aragon. And in every one of these kingdoms of the Crown it's got its own baronies, with full jurisdiction over them.

DON PEDRO: Well, that's very nice indeed! It sounds more like a province than a diocese! The bishopric could behave differently, as Livio was saying earlier. I'm amazed the bishop hasn't put down the building works in the cathedral to his own account, seeing how much income he's got and how little the cathedral chapter has.

FABIO: There's no way he'll do that! The chapter would be happy if only he gave what he's obliged to. But he won't even give that.

DON PEDRO: Maybe he's following the example of our archbishop, Tomàs de Vilanova, who died not very long ago. He preferred giving all his income to the poor — he used to say they were the living temples of God — instead of building churches, which are dead ones. Or maybe he's got a big house for servants used as a hospital or a hospice for poor gentlefolk.

FABIO: I don't see the bishop with any such servants, and I don't see him performing charity like that. Not that he hasn't got the opportunity, or indeed the duty and the ability, to do so, what with the hordes of poor beggars that there are in Tortosa these days, with this awful famine that's afflicting nearly the whole of Spain. They walk along the streets so bloated that it hurts you just to look at them. And that's not counting the host of paupers who are too ashamed to beg and are simply dying of hunger. We know for a fact that in lots of homes people are just surviving on herbs and carob beans. But I still don't see him moving a finger to do more in the way of charity than he's ever done. If he does, it's so little that it's little more than nothing.

DON PEDRO: I'm not surprised, then, that he won't pay for the works in the cathedral. Because, if he won't do what he's bound to do by law, he's hardly going to do something that's entirely voluntary.

LIVIO: Lots of people reckon that he's as duty bound to do one thing as the other. People say that one third of his income ought to be used for his personal expenses, another third for the poor, and the last for church building.

DON PEDRO: Isn't your present bishop called Ferrando de Loaces?

FABIO: That's right.

DON PEDRO: There's no need not to trust him. Even if he hasn't done anything up to now, he'll do something when least you expect it. I'm told he's wealthy, and you can always get more out of a well-heeled man than out of a down-and-out. Besides, being a learned man, he knows what his duty is. If he isn't moved by shame, he will be by conscience.

FABIO: By faith, may God enlighten him! Otherwise, this sacred and necessary building work will just have to stop, and it would be a great shame if that were to happen.

DON PEDRO: Let's leave it at that, then! There are twelve hours in a day, plenty of time to change one's mind! I'm sure he'll change his mind before too long. Tell me, Fabio, this old church over here that's to be demolished, wasn't it a mosque once upon a time? It certainly looks like one.

FABIO: Livio will know more about that than me.

LIVIO: That was never a mosque. It was built as a church after Tortosa became Christian this last time.

DON PEDRO: What? Do you mean Tortosa had been Christian before?

LIVIO: Like the rest of Spain, it once belonged to the Goths. And weren't they Christian? Of course they were, both before and after they lost Spain.

DON PEDRO: Well, by my faith, it certainly looks very old. How long ago do you suppose it was built?

LIVIO: I'll tell you. It was begun in 1158 and finished in 1178. You can see that from an inscription carved on a stone that's set into the wall near the old sacristy, near where the choir is now.

DON PEDRO: Have they got a lot of relics here?

FABIO: A fair number. And the ones they've got are in handsome reliquaries.

DON PEDRO: I'm told that divine office and church ceremonies are performed here with great pomp and ceremony.

FABIO: That's quite true. And I can tell you that, as far as that's concerned, I think this cathedral has a distinct advantage over all the others I've ever seen, and that's quite a few, because first of all here only the canons are allowed to say mass at the high altar, and usually as many as ten or a dozen chaplains take part, and for that they enjoy a special income that's enough for them to live on. On special days it's either the bishop or the dignitaries of highest rank who say mass. The deacon and the sub-deacon also have to be canons, and one or the other is a dignitary. And, when they read the Gospel and the Epistle, they're accompanied by all the chaplains who serve at the altar, together with the beadle, at the front, dressed in a long scarlet cassock with sleeves lined in purple satin, bearing a handsome gilt silver mace, and they look as if they were accompanying a bishop. At vespers, when it comes to the Magnificat, all these priests accompany the presbyter to the altar — that's to say, either the bishop or one of the other high dignitaries — with six great silver candlesticks and two censers, and the presbyter is accompanied by another canon. In the choir it's the canons who begin the service. When they display the True Cross on Passion Sunday, they're more refined and perform the most perfect and pious rites that you can see anywhere in these kingdoms. It's a splendid spectacle. And they carry out all the rituals with great perfection, especially when celebrating the festivity of Our Lady, who, as if out of gratitude, gave the cathedral a ribbon made with her own hands — the cathedral having been founded in her name and her honour — and the ribbon is looked after with great veneration and piety.

Don Pedro: Really?

Fabio: It's exactly as I say.

Livio: But wait a moment. What you're saying is really quite strange. It's pretty hard to credit. And it could even damage your reputation. After all, as you know and as the Marquis of Santillana says, one really shouldn't talk about supernatural things.

Fabio: I'm telling you that our cathedral regards it as perfectly true. On the Feast of the Holy Ribbon they celebrate a special service — it's in the breviaries in the whole diocese — in which the story of the miracle is explained in detail.

Don Pedro: So, please, let's hear the story.

Fabio: It's rather a long business, but I can show you where it comes in the breviary. Then you'll be able to read it at your leisure, as you know enough Latin. However, as we're on the subject, I'd also like to tell you about another mystery. You'll be as amazed by it as you were by the one you've just heard. Livio, do you know about the miracle of the prisoners?

Livio: Oh, that's another strange affair, and it's certainly worth hearing about.

Don Pedro: I'd like to hear it. I really enjoy hearing about the miracles God performs through the intercession of His saints.

Livio: You only say that in order not to appear to be the least bit Lutheran!

DON PEDRO: I wouldn't want, or even seem, to be anything so evil or so bestial! Fabio, please tell the story.

FABIO: Many years ago, the canons of this cathedral had two Moorish prisoners working in the bakery. Since the bakery, which was known as the Canonry, was over by the hospital, the two prisoners used to walk through the cathedral and the cloister on their way to the bishop's palace, where the canons receive their rations. Well, seeing the great piety with which the people revered the image of Our Lady on the high altar, they too got into the habit of bowing to her. Little by little, inspired by divine grace, they professed such devotion to the image that every day they begged her to deliver them from captivity, promising that, if she returned them to their homes, they'd send her two gold altar fronts, to her honour and glory. Then, one night, fourteen years after they'd been taken prisoner, they suddenly woke up and found that the irons they'd had around their ankles had disappeared. Thinking about that, and pondering it well, they promptly took some bread and two jugs of water, and, in a skiff that they found by the riverside with a couple of pairs of oars in it, they rowed out to sea and landed safely in Alexandria, the city of their birth. Once there, bearing in mind the immense favour they'd received from the Holy Lady and the offering they'd promised her, they immediately had the two finest altar fronts made that they could afford. Then, in order to prevent their neighbours finding out, and not daring to ask a sailor to deliver them, they made a box and put the two altar fronts in it, together with a message written in Arabic telling how the two prisoners from Tortosa cathedral were sending those two altar fronts for the service of Our Lady in the cathedral. And, since they had no other way of sending them to her, they begged her to make sure they'd arrive safely. In the end, the box, which they'd caulked very carefully with pitch, was washed up on the beach at Tarragona and was taken to the archbishop by some fishermen who came across it. When it was opened and its contents were seen and the message read, the archbishop sent one of the altar fronts here to Tortosa and kept the other one for Tarragona cathedral.

DON PEDRO: Oh, what a marvellous story! I'm amazed by what you've said. Not because it's hard to believe, as it's easy for Our Lady to obtain from Christ, her son and our saviour, those and even greater favours, as she does for our benefit every day. What amazes me is that God should have allowed those two prisoners to leave here, where sooner or later they could have been converted to the Christian faith and saved their souls, and let them go back to their own land where they would be in danger of losing them if they persisted in their wicked creed.

FABIO: No! Wait a moment! I haven't finished yet. A little while after all that had happened, those two prisoners found out that the two altar fronts had arrived, the way I've just told you, and seeing clearly what a great miracle had been wrought, they vowed to become Christians and go to Jerusalem to visit the Holy Sepulchre, where, serving God, they came to a good end and earned the crown of heaven.

DON PEDRO: Now I'm happy and perfectly satisfied with the story and its outcome! The only thing I'd still like to ask is how you're so certain about it all.

FABIO: The main proof we've got is the altar front itself. It's still carefully kept here in the cathedral, and it's only put on show on the day of the relics, as that's what it's held to be. And, as the memory of this miracle has been passed on from the time when it occurred until the present day, the altar front is believed to be the very one the prisoners sent. What's more, the cathedral possesses a document painted and written on a piece of parchment that's kept in a wooden panel on which everything I've told you is written, and the document was brought from Barcelona by a notary called Miquel Miravet who, in his capacity as a notary, made an affidavit concerning what he'd found and seen in Barcelona, where he'd gone on some urgent business to do with public instruments that Tortosa had sent in connection with a dire necessity relating to a war that was raging in our land. The fact is, though, that the altar front was already venerated then and was held to be the one that had been sent by the two prisoners, just as it is now. And, just to finish, let me tell you that the one that was kept in Tarragona crumbled into little pieces. In fact, hardly anyone even remembers it. And the one we've got here is like new!

DON PEDRO: May God's goodness be praised for all time! In how many different ways does He reveal to us His omnipotence, grace and mercy! Let's be off to hear mass. Look, the priest is just coming out to say it.

LIVIO: Let us, indeed! And, as you'll both be doing me the honour of dining with me, we'll have the rest of the day to carry on talking.

The Second Dialogue

THE SECOND DIALOGUE, WHICH TREATS OF THE CONQUEST
OF TORTOSA BY THE COUNT OF BARCELONA, AS WELL AS MANY
OTHER MEMORABLE MATTERS THAT ARE PLEASANT TO HEAR,
ALL OF WHICH DIGNIFY THE HONOUR OF THE CROWN OF
ARAGON, AND MOST ESPECIALLY THAT OF THE CATALAN NATION.
THE CHARACTERS ARE THE SAME AS IN THE FIRST DIALOGUE.

Speakers:
FABIO, a gentleman; DON PEDRO, a Valencian;
LIVIO, a knight.

FABIO: Now that we've had lunch, and the season isn't yet hot enough
for us to have to indulge in a siesta, let's go for a walk around the city.
Then we can go out by whichever gate we choose and take a look at
the countryside.

DON PEDRO: It will do us good to take a spot of exercise. That's if Livio
agrees.

LIVIO: Whatever you two think is best will suit me fine. I'm always happy
to go along with whatever my friends wish. I wouldn't want to do anything that they didn't.

DON PEDRO: That really is the rule of good friendship — to go along with
whatever one's friends want to do, or don't. And, as we all feel like
going for a walk, let's first go and stroll around the city, as Fabio suggests. It will do us good, as I say, because we've had too much to eat.

FABIO: Yes, exercise is very healthy, as long as it isn't overdone. It warms
you up, and that helps the digestion, and a good digestion improves
your health.

DON PEDRO: But our friend Livio goes much too far. He always
overindulges his guests. I say that in future we'll have to come to a prior
agreement with this gentleman about the amount of food he feeds us!

FABIO: Don Pedro, what you say is perfectly right. Amongst friends there's no need to overdo it like that — nor, indeed, with anyone — because too much food is bad for your digestion, tires your taste buds and does your pocket no good, either!

DON PEDRO: What you say about your pocket is spoken like a Catalan![21]

FABIO: There's no harm being careful. As the saying goes: "Even in adversity, moderation means duration."

LIVIO: I've got no idea what you're complaining about. If I've done anything wrong, it's been offering you less than I should have done, not more.

DON PEDRO: My stomach knows the truth about that! But now, leaving flattery aside, I just want to say that I don't find amongst the Catalan nation any of that stinginess, as far as serving food is concerned, that people talk about. Wherever I've been in Catalonia I've been served with great abundance and liberality, even by people who hardly knew me. As far as I can see, people regard it as just as natural as breathing.

FABIO: That's perfectly true. You should see how a knight and all his company are treated. It's a pleasure to see how happily and generously they're served and fed! And that isn't just by close friends and acquaintances. It even goes for people one's hardly even met before. I've seen that happen as often as anyone.

LIVIO: It's all the many feuding factions there are in Catalonia that make them behave like that, so that sometimes they even force their guests to eat.

DON PEDRO: I can well believe it. But tell me: where did that saying come from — how did it originate? — the one that defines stinginess by saying "It looks like a Barcelona dinner table", because in a way it sounds as though it's detrimental to Catalonia at large?

LIVIO: It's malicious people who've exploited that saying. In actual fact, it began as a way of expressing abundance, not miserliness. However, as the citizens of Barcelona have a reputation for being careful when it comes to sobriety and saving — though, speaking for myself, I don't see it that way at all, in fact I've always found them just the opposite — people have come round to thinking that that saying was invented to denote stinginess.

---

[21] Catalans had, and still have, a reputation for thrift.

DON PEDRO: Let's hear, then, why it means abundance. Please, let's hear the story!

LIVIO: To tell you the truth, if I were to start from the beginning, it would be a very long story indeed. For the present purpose, though, I'll just say that people talk about that Barcelona dinner table because Ramon Berenguer, the third count of Barcelona to bear the name[22] — in order to celebrate the entry into the city of Matildis, the wife of Emperor Henry II, who had come to Barcelona to see him and to thank him for the great favour he did her when he disproved the crime of adultery of which she'd been falsely accused — ordered tables to be set all the way from the castle of Montcada to Barcelona, which is roughly two leagues, and had them all laid out with all kinds of food and with the same fine wines as for the table at which the Empress herself ate. And it's from that great abundance and extraordinary generosity that the saying derives.

DON PEDRO: I like it! That must indeed be the origin. It's amazing how many pithy sayings there are in Catalonia, and how much they're used! It's astonishing! In politics, one could live by them just as well as by the counsels of Aristotle or Cicero. There's no question about it: the Catalan nation is courteous, brave and wise, even though nowadays — like the Aragonese and the Valencians — it's been stuck in a corner by those Castilians who want everything for themselves.

LIVIO: It's hardly surprising. There are lots of them, and they're stronger than us. That's why they can rally to the king better than we can. As the Marquis of Santillana says in his *Proverbs*, men who are present are better regarded than those who aren't. It's perfectly natural, and you can see it any day of the week. The world turns upside down, and the ascendancy of nations shifts from one to another, never staying long with any one of them. As Solomon says in the last chapter of *Ecclesiastes*: "There's nothing new under the sun." And, as Terence says: "All things are subject to change."[23] Experience teaches us that it's like that with regard to everything. Especially where brilliance, fame and glory are concerned, one day they're ruled by one nation, the next day by another. And it's just as true of major matters as it is of minor ones: there's nothing that lasts forever. You can see it in the first of all monarchies — the Chaldean and Assyrian one —

---

22 The reference is to Count Ramon Berenguer III, 'the Great' (1082-1131).
23 In the original, cited in Latin.

which was overcome and defeated by the Medes and the Persians.
They were defeated by the Greeks, and the Greeks by the Romans.
And, even though it may look as if the Romans still rule the world, to
tell you the truth it doesn't look like that to me. What we see today of
the Roman Empire is, at the most, a mere shadow of its past. As for
Spain, we've been as restless and changeable as any other part of the
world. The first people who settled here, at the time of Tubal,[24] were
beaten by the Egyptians, the Egyptians by the Greeks, the Greeks by
the Celts, the Celts by the Phoenicians, the Phoenicians by the
Carthaginians, the Carthaginians by the Romans, the Romans by the
Vandals, the Suebi, the Alani and others, and they by the Goths, the
Goths by the Moors or Saracens, and the Saracens, here in Catalonia,
by the Germans and the Franks. Which is why, if now we see the
Castilians ruling the roost, tomorrow we'll see how they're ruled over
themselves, as they were at other times, and their boasting won't
make the slightest bit of difference.

FABIO: Yes, they talk big, which is why lots of people say the only good
things that come from Castile are those that are dumb.

DON PEDRO: What kind of dumb things?

FABIO: Horses, mules, oxen, sheep... And it's true — their cattle actually are better than ours.

DON PEDRO: That's a witty reply!

LIVIO: On top of that, they've got something that's even worse, which
is that they're so despotic. They believe that everything they have is
the best, and that what other people have is the worst. It's as if they'd
dropped from heaven, and the rest of mankind had crawled out of
the mud. The odd thing is that, if history is to be believed, there isn't
a single nation in Spain that's always been so blinkered and dull as
the Castilians. They've hardly ever gone beyond their frontiers, not
just to rule others, but even to make war on other kingdoms, as the
Crowns of Aragon and Portugal have done. If you want proof, there's
the islands of the Mediterranean for you — Sicily, Sardinia, Majorca,
Menorca, Ibiza, Corsica — and the kingdom of Naples, all of which
were conquered by Alfonso of Aragon,[25] and there's the campaign
recounted by Ramon Muntaner that took the Catalans to

---

[24] According to legend, Tubal, a grandson of Noah, was the first settler in the Iberian
Peninsula.
[25] Alfonso V of Aragon, known as 'the Magnanimous' (1396-1458).

Constantinople, where they stayed and performed so many feats, not just for their own honour and glory, but for all of Spain.[26] As for Portugal, there's all her possessions in the Atlantic Ocean.

In Spain itself, most times when the Castilians have fought their Christian neighbours they've been soundly beaten. And in the main battles they've fought with the Moors, if they've won it's because we've fought by their side. If you want proof, just listen to this. The battle against the mighty king of Cordova, which was fought near that city at the time of King Alfonso V of Leon and Count Sancho of Castile, was won thanks to the might and ingenuity of Count Ramon Borrell of Barcelona. The city of Toledo, when it fell to Alfonso VI, was conquered thanks to the courage and skill in matters of war of Sancho I of Aragon. The taking of Almeria, in the reign of Alfonso VIII of Castile, was due, not to the king, who did hardly anything, but to Count Ramon Berenguer IV of Barcelona. The city of Cuenca was won by Alfonso I of Aragon on his own in order to please that same Alfonso VIII of Castile. The great battle of El Muladar, near Las Navas de Tolosa, was won by the good counsel, effort and bravery of Pedro I of Aragon, whom the Aragonese call Pedro II. The battle of El Salado, fought against the kings of the Benemerines, Béjaïa, Tunis and Granada near the rock of El Ciervo at the time of Alfonso XI of Castile, was won thanks to the courage of Pedro III of Aragon, known to the Aragonese as Pedro IV, who sent Mossèn Pere de Montcada with ten well armed galleys, which served him skilfully at sea and were mainly responsible for the victory on land. And, in the conquest of Algeciras by that same King Alfonso, it was that same King Pedro who distinguished himself the most.[27]

DON PEDRO: I don't recall reading in the history of that king that he went there in person.

LIVIO: Diego de Valera, who is a Castilian, says so, and he wouldn't have said something in our favour if it weren't true. Finally, the kingdom of Granada — which, as you know, had always been a thorn in the flesh of the kingdom of Castile — could never be conquered until King

---

[26] See *The Catalan Expedition to the East: from the Chronicle of Ramon Muntaner*, translated by Robert D. Hughes (Barcelona/Woodbridge, Barcino/Tamesis, 2006).

[27] The Catalan expedition to the Moorish city of Cordova took place in 1010; Toledo was conquered from the Moors in 1085; Almeria, in 1147; and Cuenca, in 1177. The battle of Las Navas de Tolosa was fought in 1212; the battle of El Salado, in 1340; and Algeciras was conquered in 1344.

Ferdinand of Aragon took care of it. And the expedition across the ocean to the Indies, begun by the Genoese Christopher Columbus and finished off by Hernán Cortés and Francisco Pizarro, was undertaken on the command and orders, and with the good fortune, of that same King Ferdinand, and had nothing to do with the Castilians.

DON PEDRO: You've explained all that very well, and it's worth thinking about it seriously, but I don't follow what you say about the Aragonese calling the First Second, and the Third Fourth!

LIVIO: Let me explain. Before Catalonia was joined to Aragon, the Aragonese had a king called Peter and another one called Alfonso, and they counted them as the first of the kings who bore those names once the two kingdoms had been united. The Catalans, however, don't count those first ones, because they didn't reign over Catalonia. They only count those who bore those names after the unification. So they call Ildefonso, the son of Count Ramon Berenguer, Alfonso I, even though there had been an Alfonso I of Aragon; and they call Peter, Ildefonso's son, Peter I, even though there had been a previous King Peter in Aragon.

DON PEDRO: Now I see! So why don't you get back to what you were saying, which was really very interesting?

LIVIO: Moving on, then, if we take a look at the towns in the kingdom of Old Castile when Spain was conquered by the Moors, we can see that they were the weakest and the easiest ones to take. On this point, I've heard it said by some trustworthy Aragonese knights that, when the marquis of Vélez — a well-read man — passed through Saragossa, he told them that he owned a reliable Arabic history of the conquest of Spain which said that the biggest difficulties and the greatest dangers that the Moors had to face were in this province of Tarragona, not in Baetica or Carpetania, which are now Old and New Castile, and that, after winning the great battle against King Roderick, they conquered every place they came across there without meeting any serious resistance.[28] We also read that, when Augustus conquered Spain, he came up against the biggest hardships, difficulties and dangers in Celtiberia, which was the main reason why he wanted his name to be perpetuated there, and not in any other province in

---

[28] The reference is to the battle of Guadalete (711/712), lost by Roderick, known as the last king of the Goths. It opened the way for the Moors to conquer Toledo, the Visigothic capital of Spain.

Spain, and had it incorporated into the city of Saragossa, which to this day is still known in Latin as *Caesar Augusta*.

Which is why I just don't understand why those Castilians are so arrogant. I can tell you: I just can't stand it, especially when I see them put on such insufferably outrageous airs, not just in the way they speak, but in the way they write, too. If you don't believe me, just take a look at what Juan Sedeño writes in his *Suma de varones ilustres* and you'll see that he has no problem talking about the deeds of some kings of Castile which, for anyone who knows what really happened, sound more like a joke than anything else. For the sake of his own nation's honour, it would have been better if he'd said nothing at all. He ought to have realised that, instead of talking about kings just because they were kings, what mattered was whether they were famous. Something else he does, just to fill up space and spin out the number of Castilians in his *Suma*, is stick in the deeds of ordinary people which sound like old wives' tales or farce. And, in order to avoid granting glory or honour to any Spaniard who wasn't a Castilian, he's left out the memorable deeds of lots of Spanish kings, especially kings of the Crown of Aragon and counts of Barcelona who weren't just the equals of the most outstanding kings of Castile but, in my opinion, were quite clearly superior.

DON PEDRO: From what you say, he only talks about the Castilians, and they think they're the only people in the world.

LIVIO: That's right. He talks about over two hundred, belonging to many different nations — some quite rightly, but others not at all.[29]

DON PEDRO: So who were those kings and counts that you think he should have mentioned, but doesn't?

LIVIO: Oh! There are so many that, were I to try and count them, I'd be more of a bore than Juan Sedeño was disrespectful!

DON PEDRO: Just tell us some of them — the first that spring to mind — and, if they really were important, that will be enough for us to appreciate just how careless that Castilian author is.

LIVIO: If that's what you want, I'll tell you. First of all, he leaves out all mention of King James I.[30] His great deeds, virtue and valour can't be crammed into a short summary. He conquered three kingdoms:

---

[29] Sedeño's *Suma* deals with 224 illustrious men, not one of whom came from the Crown of Aragon.

[30] James I of Aragon, 'the Conqueror' (1208-1276).

Valencia, Majorca and Murcia. And he went to the council that met
in France where a lot of Christian princes discussed the defence and
aggrandisement of Christendom, and did and said things there that
shouldn't be forgotten.

DON PEDRO: Holy Mary! You mean he doesn't even mention that good,
saintly and valorous king of ours?

LIVIO: Not once! Nor does he mention Peter II, whom the Aragonese
call Peter III and, like the French, call him Peter the Great.[31] He was
one of the most notable men ever. The Pope and the king of Naples
conspired against him, as did almost the whole of Christendom, but
he prevailed and triumphed over them all, winning from them the
island of Sicily, which was his by his wife Constança, throwing out
King Charles of Naples, who had occupied it. He also performed
great exploits in Africa, where he won stunning victories. Sedeño
also leaves out Alfonso IV, whom the Aragonese call Alfonso V, and
who was also known as Alfonso of Naples.[32] Apart from being the wisest and most magnanimous monarch of his time, he conquered the
kingdom of Naples, and Apulia and Calabria, which were actually his
by right. He subdued the people of Florence and Pisa, became military commander of the Church and the most feared and beloved
amongst all the princes in the whole world.

Sedeño also misses out lots of the other kings of Spain — kings of
the Crowns of Aragon, Navarre and Portugal — who, thanks to their
famous deeds, deserve mention a lot more than some of the kings of
Castile that he includes and whose names I'll omit in order not to
embarrass their forebears. Nor does he mention that most famous
and invincible prince, Count Ramon Berenguer III of Barcelona.[33]
He didn't just win Majorca the first time, when the Genoese and the
Pisans, in whose care he'd left it, sold it back to the Moors for a sum
of money. He also subdued Valencia, Tortosa and Lleida, which paid
him tribute up to the end of his days. As I've mentioned before, he
also performed that most noble feat, worthy of eternal remembrance, to the glory of the whole of Spain, but most particularly of
our Catalonia, of going into single combat in order to save Matildis,
the wife of Emperor Henry II, from the false accusation of adultery,

---

31 Peter the Great (1239-1285), James I's successor.
32 Alfonso V, 'the Magnanimous' (1396-1458).
33 Ramon Berenguer the Great (1082-1131).

leaving one of her accusers dead on the field and forcing the other to disavow all that he'd said against her.

DON PEDRO: And how did the count happen to be present on that occasion?

LIVIO: He went there specially from here in Catalonia just in order to perform that saintly, pious and brave deed, and he went with just one companion, Beltran de Rocabruna, from Provence, knowing as he did that there were two accusers. But Rocabruna discovered how fierce the accusers were and, the night before the battle, he disappeared, leaving the count in the lurch, but the valorous count didn't flinch one bit. As I say, he fought fearlessly and achieved total victory.

DON PEDRO: I'm surprised that the count did that before being absolutely certain whether the accusation against the empress was true or false. After all, in cases like that it's very important to have good grounds for dispute.

LIVIO: As a matter of fact, he was absolutely certain about it.

DON PEDRO: How's that?

LIVIO: By the most elegant and ingenious guile that's ever been heard of. It was like this. He pretended to be a priest who lived a very saintly life, and that's how he obtained the information that the empress was a most devout lady. When he got to the emperor's court in Germany, he managed to speak to her, and their conversation turned into an act of confession which enabled him to see how pure she was and what liars her wicked accusers were, which is what made him decide to go ahead with the deed, from which he emerged with the glory and the honour that I've told you about.

DON PEDRO: How marvellous! That really deserves never to be forgotten.

FABIO: Being a Catalan, as I am, I'm absolutely delighted to have heard that. Which is why, Livio, you'd do me a great favour if you told us the whole story in detail. It really wouldn't do to leave out a single iota of such an exceptional and heroic deed.

LIVIO: It's a long story to tell. You can read it in the *Life* of the count, and it's told by lots of other historians, so both of you can read it at your leisure whenever you like. However, Pedro Mexía did what you'd expect of a Castilian and left out of his history of the emperors the fact that this glorious act was carried out by the count. He just says that somehow or other the empress's innocence came to light, without explaining how. And I reckon he decided to put it like that simply because Ramon Berenguer wasn't a Castilian.

DON PEDRO: And doesn't Sedeño say *anything* about that pious and learned prince?

LIVIO: Not a thing! Nor does he mention Ramon Berenguer IV, the count's son and heir, who was the handsomest, noblest and most magnanimous of princes, fortunate in battle and the wisest in matters of war and peace of all the princes of his time throughout the entire world.[34] It would take a long time to explain all his doings — conquering Almeria, Tortosa and ancient and populous Lleida — or to spell out all the details regarding those last two cities. In fact, he extended the frontiers of Catalonia more than any of his predecessors, and he built three hundred churches to honour the glorious name of Jesus Christ.

DON PEDRO: Is that the count who married Petronila, the daughter and heiress to King Ramiro of Aragon, the king with the bell?[35]

LIVIO: Yes, that's the one.

DON PEDRO: I've always heard what a very singular prince he was. And didn't that wretched writer like even *him* enough to put him in his *Suma de varones ilustres*? Throw the fellow to the ravens!

LIVIO: Those Castilian historians are nearly all the same. To avoid publicising the glory of those Spaniards who aren't Castilian, they just leave out the truth, and to glorify their own nation they don't think twice about telling lies, and it makes no difference whether they're talking about great deeds or small ones. Look at Florián de Ocampo! With all his typical pomposity and gravitas, he doesn't hesitate to declare in his histories that King Philip, the Emperor Charles' father, was king of Spain just because he was king of Castile, ignoring the authority of the Catholic King Ferdinand, who at the time ruled Aragon and Granada, or King Manuel of Portugal, or King John of Labrit who ruled Navarre, all of which kingdoms make up the greater part of Spain. What's more, nearly all Castilian historiographers insist on saying 'Castile' when they mean the whole of Spain. Pero Mexia, in the second chapter of his life of Emperor Maximilian in his *Coronica imperial*, does even worse. He has the kingdom of Naples as

34 Ramon Berenguer IV, known as 'the Holy' (c. 1113-1162).
35 According to legend, Ramiro II snuffed out a rebellion by his noblemen by inviting them to Huesca to listen to a bell that, he said, would be heard throughout the kingdom, and promptly had the twelve most important nobles decapitated.

a dominion of the Crown of Castile, being, as it obviously is, part of
the Crown of Aragon, as even little children know!

DON PEDRO: How could he not know that? Anyone with only half an eye
could see that the king's royal coat of arms shows the arms of Naples
perfectly clearly in the quarter of the arms of Aragon, not Castile.

LIVIO: If they cast doubt on facts that are perfectly obvious, just imagine
what they do with ones that aren't!

FABIO: That's absolutely true! Just ask the Catalan nation! They'll tell
you better than anyone.

DON PEDRO: Why?

FABIO: Because it was during the conquest of the kingdom of Naples,
in the service of the king who conquered it — who was Alfonso IV
of Aragon, whose rights were inherited by the Catholic King Ferdinand — that deeds were done that were as heroic as any that the
Romans performed at the height of their ascendancy. In particular,
one, the most singular and most worthy of remembrance of any that
I've ever heard of. No, I've never heard of another like it.

DON PEDRO: You've praised it so much, Fabio, that we must hear what
it was.

FABIO: I haven't sung its praises as much as it deserves, but if you listen
you'll see that what I say is perfectly true. It's well known that Joan,
queen of Naples in her own right, adopted King Alfonso of Aragon,
and that, having given him the kingdom, he went there, and that,
when she revoked the adoption and the gift of the kingdom, the king
had to take up arms against the duke of Anjou, whom the queen had
later adopted as her son and to whom she had given the kingdom.
The war between them was raging, and lots of events took place,
because it was very long. Sometimes things went well for the king,
and sometimes they didn't. In particular, on one occasion the king
was forced to take refuge in one of the fortresses of that kingdom,
called Castelnuovo, without enough forces or means to defend himself, let alone to get out of that predicament.

Finding himself, then, in such a fix, he had to send for help to these
kingdoms of the Crown, and he particularly approached Catalonia.
Realising how urgent the king's needs were, the principality of
Catalonia called a meeting of the parliament in Barcelona to debate
how help could be sent. And, whilst they did their best to bring about
what they wanted with all the sympathy in the world, they couldn't
agree on how to do it, as the Generalitat of Catalonia can't make an

extraordinary budget unless it's proposed by the Corts in the presence of the king. And, seeing how it was impossible for the Corts to meet, as the king couldn't be present, and the need was pressing, a solution to the problem was discussed in the midst of all those complications. As I've already told you, it was the strangest solution that's ever been heard of, and it was this: that an eminent and distinguished embassy be sent to the king, to be accompanied by six or seven thousand men, made up of knights and foot soldiers well armed for war, in a suitable fleet of ships and galleys to escort and guard the ambassadors who were to be sent to the king. And they, in the name and on the part of the entire principality of Catalonia, were to present him with the reply that no constitutional means had been found to come to his Majesty's aid. However, as they'd travelled all the way there in order to deliver that negative reply, were he to wish to make use of them and their escort, they were entirely at his service. And that's what happened, and that's how the embassy was put to the king, and the ambassadors stayed there and served and supported the king so manfully that within a short space of time he was able to leave the place where he'd been holed up and defeat his enemies and, finally, become lord of the entire kingdom quite peacefully.

DON PEDRO: So what they couldn't do directly they did in a roundabout sort of way, and all in order not to fail to come to the service and defence of their king. By my life, what an unusual and delectable feat that was! You were perfectly right to make so much of it. I, at least, have never read anything like it.

FABIO: That's how it is. And what's most amazing is that aid was brought to the king in under thirty days from his requesting it.

DON PEDRO: That sounds impossible to me.

FABIO: That's what I used to think, too, but that's what Friar Gaubert Fabricio de Vagad, the chronicler of the Crown of Aragon, says, and he's regarded as very reliable, and some people say help arrived even sooner.

LIVIO: Yes, it all happened just as Fabio says, and it's for that reason, and thanks to an untold number of other feats that our nation performed in that campaign, that the Catalans won singular fame in the city of Naples, and there's a Catalan Street there to prove it. But, going back to what I was saying about the ways of the Castilians, that same Sedeño makes a big thing of some Castilian knights who threw a spear at a bull, but he doesn't say anything about the outstanding feats and deeds performed at all times by innumerable knights of the Crown of Aragon and, in modern times, by Don Ramon de Cardona and Don Hugo de Montcada, who were equal to the greatest soldiers in Spain.[36] He could have learned about their doings without any trouble at all, without even consulting books. And he also decided to forget about those two glorious exploits carried out by Don Felip de Cervelló when he went to the aid of Milan and Pavia, but for which both cities would have been lost.[37]

DON PEDRO: That's probably because he didn't want to mention the Castilian captain who accompanied Don Felip and who refused to join him in the attack on Pavia until he was almost forced to.

LIVIO: That may well be. They never cease to accuse Don Hugo de Montcada of being defeated because he took bad advice and was arrogant, and they only do that in order to cover up the lack of courage and the mischief on the part of the Castilian captains of two of Don Hugo's galleys. It's absolutely certain and perfectly well known that, if they'd attacked instead of turning tail, Don Hugo would have been victorious.[38]

DON PEDRO: Actually, I've always heard say that Hugo was unlucky in everything he tried.

LIVIO: I've heard that, too, but from Castilians, who were mortally envious of him. And, even if we were to think the same, he was still the most prudent and astute, the boldest and mightiest soldier of his day, and he was amongst those who had the best judgement in matters of war and peace. He did everything a good soldier could do and advise in all that he undertook. If, none the less, he wasn't always successful, that wasn't his fault, because, as you know, it's the commander's business to give the orders and supply the means for battle, but, as good Catholics, we're bound to believe that victory is in God's hands alone. Heathens, on the other hand, attribute victory simply to good fortune. Although fortune didn't favour him, the proof of Don Hugo's valour can be seen perfectly well in the way he began and ended his career. He left the castle of Aitona, that belonged to his

[36] Ramon de Cardona, viceroy of Sicily (1507-1509) and of Naples (1509-1522); Hugo de Montcada, viceroy of Sicily (1509-1516) and of Naples (1527).

[37] Felip de Cervelló, viceroy of Majorca (1538-1547).

[38] Blockaded in Naples by the Genoese and French fleets in 1528, Hugo de Montcada was killed when his fleet tried to break out, and most of his ships were captured or sunk. He was closely related to the dedicatee of Despuig's *Dialogues*.

father, Don Pedro de Montcada, with only a hundred ducats and two servants and a horse and a hack, which was all his father could afford, and when he died he had an income of twenty-four thousand ducats a year and, what's more, was viceroy of Naples and general commanding Italy and Africa for our king, the Emperor Charles V, who, when any Castilians denigrated what Don Hugo did, used to say that he was as prudent, wise, valorous and singular a soldier as any in his day. So you may be sure that everything that's been said against him comes from the bad feeling and pure envy that they have towards us, because we're freer than them, which is why they'd like to deprive us of everything we've got and why they think we do them wrong if we don't worship them.

What do you think? Most Castilians actually dare to say out loud that this province of ours isn't Spain and that, therefore, we aren't true Spaniards, and the blessed sinners don't realise how wrong and how ignorant they are, and how blinded they are by envy and malice, for this province isn't just Spain: it's the best Spain, and it's always been held up as such by every nation that has reached our shores. If you go back to the earliest times, when Spain was called Celtiberia, we were regarded as warlike and utterly invincible. Then, when the Romans called us Hispania Tarraconensis or Hispania Citerior, we were thought of as a flaming torch of war, either for or against Rome, the force and the power that enabled them to tame the rest of the provinces of Spain, and others beyond. And if you look at modern times, tell me what Spanish province has outdone the Crown of Aragon, and in particular our Catalonia, on land or at sea? It's so obvious, so evident, that there's no man, however ignorant he be, who doesn't know it. And the Castilians know it, too. But, simply in order not to give us our due, they don't just ignore it, but deny it. God alone knows whether they're the cause of many of the ills that wouldn't exist, if it weren't for them. But just look what they've done in Ostia. After the Spaniards had won it, two Castilian captains treacherously returned it to the Pope.[39] My friends, if I were to tell you everything I know, I could prove to you perfectly clearly that all the discord that exists between the Pope and King Philip has been caused by Castilians. But let's leave it at that. There's no point just going on and on.

---

39 The reference may be to the fall of Ostia to the Spanish general, Gonzalo Fernández de Córdoba, in 1496.

DON PEDRO: The fact is you'd never finish. There's so much to say.

FABIO: So, Livio, what you were saying is that the count who married Petronila conquered our city of Tortosa?

LIVIO: Precisely.

FABIO: I take great pleasure from the fact that, thanks to that courtly prince, we were established in such a pleasant place. We really ought to honour his memory.

LIVIO: That's quite true. We do very little about it. I once told the city representatives and councillors that they ought to set up a fine statue of him at the end of the council chamber to remind people of the good deeds he did for us.

DON PEDRO: That would be an excellent idea. Barcelona has got statues of all the counts who ruled her before the emperor. Tortosa could well have a statue of the man who saved her from the followers of Mahomet.

FABIO: How long ago was it conquered?

LIVIO: It was conquered on 30 December 1148, the vespers of St. Silvester, and now we're in 1557, so it was wrested from the Moors four hundred and nine years ago.

DON PEDRO: Was it hard to conquer? Did it take very long?

LIVIO: It certainly was hard, and it took notable acts of war, as the Moors defended it very bravely. And, after they lost the city, they regrouped with all their goods in La Suda, and they had to be removed from there by force of arms six months after the siege of the city began. On 1 July of the year I mentioned, the count's navy, and that of the Genoese, sailed in — a total of 83 galleys, all together 260 different kinds of ships and vessels — and the siege was laid two days later.

DON PEDRO: What did La Suda refer to? Was it a part of the city that was easier to defend than the rest?

LIVIO: No, La Suda is what they called the castles that are still here. They were easy to defend against the lances and shields that were in use at that time.

FABIO: So how did they take it? By force of arms?

LIVIO: Where there's a strong force, a stronger force will overcome it. You know how the saying goes: "The rock is strong, but stronger still is he who knocks it down." This is what happened. When, as I was saying, the city had been taken by the Christians, a few days after it had been besieged, the Moors withdrew to the castles of La Suda, which are up there on the rocks in the middle of the city like a promontory. To the eastern side are those heights that we call Les Bastides, over which the walls pass that enclose the city, and nearby is a tower that was once a windmill. In between those heights and the castle there was a space that was some eighty-four arm's lengths wide and some sixty-four deep, and the Christians carefully and quickly filled it up with enough fagots and earth to bring it to the level of the heights and the castles. When they'd done that, the Christians set up a wooden castle, and they brought it up to the wall of the first castle of La Suda by means of ingenious devices, and they fought from there with great vigour and fury. But one third of the wooden castle was destroyed by the innumerable great rocks that the Moors shot at it with machines, some of them weighing over two hundred pounds. When the Christians saw that, they repaired the wooden castle and built on top of it a net made of thick hempen rope to protect themselves from the stones that the Moors shot at them, and that's how they renewed the combat, and they did so with such ferocity that they broke into the first castle and then easily went on to take the other two, as all three are enclosed inside the same ramparts.

DON PEDRO: How many men do you reckon that wooden castle could have held?

LIVIO: They put three hundred well-picked men in it.

DON PEDRO: Holy Mary! It held that many?

LIVIO: What's so amazing about that? The Romans and the Carthaginians placed forty men on an elephant. So why couldn't they put three hundred on a wooden contraption that they could build as big as they liked?

DON PEDRO: Do the books say whether any knight stood out in particular in the capture of those castles?

LIVIO: The chronicles of Count Ramon Berenguer tell how Mossèn Guillem Ramon de Montcada and Mossèn Pere de Sentmenat were the first to scale the walls, and that's why the count awarded them the Siege Crown and gave them two of the three castles. However, the Genoese chronicle that tells of the conquest of Tortosa and Almeria says that La Suda wasn't taken by force of arms but by a pact, and that it went like this.[40]

When the Moors had lost the city and retreated to La Suda, they sent for help to all the other Moors in Valencia, Aragon and even

---

[40] The Genoese chronicle alluded to here is the *Annales Ianuenses* of Caffaro di Caschifellone.

Catalonia, where there were also plenty. Help was offered, but it didn't arrive, and the Christians kept on fighting stubbornly, so they decided to negotiate a treaty. If, within forty days, the relief they were expecting didn't arrive, they'd surrender the castles of La Suda to the count on condition that he didn't take prisoner any of the Moors who wished to go and live elsewhere. And, in order to guarantee the pact, they gave the count a hundred of their most important men as hostages. And, as the relief they were expecting never turned up, they gave the castles to the count, as they'd agreed.

As I say, that's what the Genoese chronicle states. I don't know which version is the more likely, though all the sources agree that the city itself was taken by force of arms. The count's own chronicle, which speaks of the campaign at greater length, says that four knights won the Siege Crown in the taking of Tortosa because all four of them entered by the wall that nowadays goes from the turret near the castle to the monastery of Santo Domingo, and that they fought their way till they reached what was known as the house of La Suda, in the street that's still called La Suda Street today, and which is now owned by a man named Llorenç Gomis. On the corner of that house, on the wall that looks out towards the castle gate, which in those days was part of a square, the count ordered the arms of those four knights of his to be carved in stone, and they're still there to this day.

FABIO: I've seen them there often enough, but I think they've been moved to the front of the house.

LIVIO: That's quite right.

DON PEDRO: And why were they moved?

LIVIO: Because the owner of the house wanted to rebuild it, and in order to make a good job of it he decided to knock down the front and the side where the arms were. And, as the square where they used to be no longer exists, and instead there's a narrow lane that climbs up Chaplains' Hill towards the castle windows, after obtaining the agreement and permission of the count of Aitona and the other knights who have an interest in the matter, he had those same arms set in the front wall, which is where they are now, even though the builder made the mistake of putting the arms of Sentmenat next to those of Montcada, instead of putting them last, which is how they had been before.

FABIO: That doesn't matter much.

DON PEDRO: It matters a lot, as they must have been placed in that order for a good reason.

LIVIO: Don Pedro is quite right, but that's the way they are now.

DON PEDRO: Who, by your life, were those four knights?

LIVIO: The first one was Mossèn Guillem Ramon de Montcada, who was the count's general on that campaign and one of the most important soldiers to come from the house of Montcada. The second one was Mossèn Berenguer de Pallars; the third, Mossèn Roger Despuig; and the fourth and last, Mossèn Pere de Sentmenat.

DON PEDRO: The feat was indeed remarkable, and it must have been greatly appreciated by the count of Barcelona, if he wanted it to be recorded by such a solid and durable memorial as those arms sculpted on the wall.

LIVIO: And it wasn't badly rewarded, either. He gave one third of the city to Montcada, as well as one of the three castles; to Pallars he gave the district of Ossera; to Despuig, the castle and the village of Paüls and the tower of Llaber and a house in the city near the Rose Gate which, together with the tower, the men of that name still possess. However, the house twice left their ownership for certain reasons, though now finally it's theirs again and today, as I say, they own it. And to Sentmenat he gave another of the three castles of La Suda and the castle and town of Casles, known today as Carles. And all those castles and towns lie within the general boundaries of Tortosa.

FABIO: How the world goes round! May the name of almighty God be praised for all time! Don't you see that only one of the lineages of those four honourable knights is left in this city, and it's Despuig? You were quite right, Livio, when you said that nothing is solid and lasting in this world.

DON PEDRO: It may well be that only one of those four houses is left here, but it's well known that there are still a lot of important members of those families in Catalonia.

LIVIO: Don Pedro, you're quite right. Only the Pallars have disappeared completely. And the oldest branch of the Despuigs, which was in Roussillon, died out over a hundred and fifty years ago. It's from them that the house of Despuig here derives. Their arms all have the same design and colours, namely: *Gules issuant from base a Mount ensigned by a Fleur-de-Lis Or.*[41] And from that house there issued the five or six main branches in the kingdom of Valencia, one of

---

[41] In the original, the Mount is *Puig* (meaning 'peak') and stands for *Despuig*, the author's family name.

which has an income from its vassals of five or six thousand ducats a year. It's the branch of Don Pedro Despuig, lord of Alcantara. And the branches in Majorca also derive from the one here, and today they own plenty of property on the island. Actually, the Perpignan branch hasn't died out altogether, because one of the barons of Oms became the head of the house when he married the sole heiress on condition that their descendents took up the name and the coat of arms of the Despuigs. To this day his issue bear the surname Oms i Despuig and the Despuig arms.

FABIO: But they didn't keep them entirely, as they were supposed to.

LIVIO: Not completely, it's true, but they do still bear their arms and they do sign their name Oms i Despuig on documents and official papers. Don Nofre d'Oms still does so today, as a descendent of the house of Despuig, and he's got good reason to do so, as he's told me more than once, because the best part of his possessions come from that house.

DON PEDRO: If that's the case, he's duty bound to do so.

LIVIO: Yes, indeed, even though nowadays it isn't worth as much as it was once upon a time. Time was when, I can tell you, the house of Despuig had a thousand vassals in the county of Roussillon.

DON PEDRO: That was a very pretty fortune.

LIVIO: It's a fact, and it's well known up there. Just one town of theirs, Tatzó d'Avall, had over eight hundred houses, though now it's deserted. They also owned Puigsotrer, Ausselló and other villages. And the spring of Salses that's so well known for the fishing also belonged to them.

FABIO: In other words, they ended up just like the rest. As they say, it's an ill wind that blows nobody any good.

DON PEDRO: About the house of Montcada — was it very distinguished in Catalonia?

FABIO: You could say it was extremely distinguished, in terms both of quantity and quality. But here's Livio, who I think must know more about it, from what he's read and heard people say.

LIVIO: It's a fact that the Montcadas were a most noble family, not just in Catalonia, but throughout Spain and France. It's always produced prominent and famous soldiers and administrators, as well as very important prelates in the Church, and leading officials in the royal household. There's no doubt about it.

DON PEDRO: For sure, it still enjoys great honour and repute.

LIVIO: Yes, but, compared with foregone times, you could say that now it's next to nothing. If only it were! Leaving aside the question of quality, which never changes, in terms of quantity, as regards its estates, it's been reduced to hardly anything, if you reckon what it used to be and how it's declined. The Montcadas were lords of the barony of Montcada, as well as of Granollers and nearly the whole of the Vallès region. They were counts of Ampurias, viscounts of Castellbò, barons of Llagostera, lords of Tortosa and Fraga and lots of other castles in Catalonia. In addition, they were counts of Foix and princes of Béarn, in France, and, besides, in Catalonia they had over two hundred and fifty tenants in their castles, towns and fortified farms.

DON PEDRO: That's really amazing! And do the Montcadas still own any of the lands you've mentioned?

LIVIO: Not a thing. Not so much as the embattlements of a castle.

DON PEDRO: And doesn't what the count of Aitona owns come from there?[42]

LIVIO: No. What he owns in Catalonia comes from the dowry that Constança of Aragon, daughter of King Peter I, brought when she married Mossèn Guillem Ramon de Montcada. And she wasn't illegitimate, as some say, but quite legitimate, though she was the issue of a secret marriage. His possessions in Aragon come partly from the pact arranged by the Montcada who brought about the marriage of Petronila and the count of Barcelona, and partly from the exchange of Tortosa for some other towns that he agreed with James II. His property in Valencia comes partly via marriage and partly from what his ancestors won during the conquest of that kingdom.

FABIO: Good God! What enormous changes of fortune — first losing so much and then managing to survive so well! It's obvious that God doesn't abandon him, but holds him firmly by the hand.

LIVIO: In regard to what you've just said, Fabio, about surviving so well, let me tell you what I was told, years ago, by a secretary of Count John, the father of the present count of Aitona, Francisco. The duke of Bavaria told a servant of Countess Anna de Cardona, Count Francisco's mother:

You should know that, after Count John died, his wife, the countess, decided to send a servant to the court of the then emperor in Germany to request certain things of him that mattered to her, with

---

[42] It should be borne in mind that the *Dialogues* are dedicated to the count of Aitona.

the order that he make the most of the favourable offices of the duke of Bavaria, as head of the house of Montcada—as it really does derive from the house of Bavaria—and he took him letters from the countess herself. And when he asked the favour and explained how Dapifer of Bavaria, who later became known as Montcada, had founded this house here in Catalonia, the duke answered, in his own language: "I was aware of the fact that Dapifer left my house, but I didn't know what had become of him, and I'm pleased to hear that they've done so well down there."

DON PEDRO: What you've said, Livio, is of no little interest or concern. It's hardly surprising that, given the authority acquired by such a noble house, we can see Montcada Streets in almost every city and village in Catalonia, named in homage to that house, and the same goes for Valencia and other towns there.

LIVIO: That's quite true. Now, do you see those knights just coming over towards us? I think they must have recognised Don Pedro and want to pay him their respects.

FABIO: I expect so, and it's a pity, because it's going to break the thread of our conversation, and I was just about to ask Livio I can't remember what else it was that I wanted to know.

DON PEDRO: It can wait till they've gone. I don't think they'll keep me talking very long.

LIVIO: Don Pedro is quite right.

The Third Dialogue

THE THIRD DIALOGUE, WHICH TREATS OF THE PRIVILEGES
AND FREEDOMS OF TORTOSA AND THE REASONS WHY THEY WERE
SO GENEROUSLY GRANTED. MENTION IS ALSO MADE OF THE
BENEFITS BESTOWED UPON OTHER KNIGHTS BY THE COUNT
OF BARCELONA DURING THE CONQUEST OF TORTOSA, AND OF
HOW, THANKS TO THE GOOD COUNSEL AND DILIGENCE OF THE
CITY'S WOMEN, IT WAS DEFENDED AGAINST THE MOORS
WHO HAD LAID SIEGE TO IT.

Speakers:
FABIO, a gentleman; DON PEDRO, a Valencian;
LIVIO, a knight.

FABIO: Livio, just so that it doesn't slip my mind — and, to be honest, my
memory isn't as good as it ought to be — I want to ask you the question I was going to put to you just before those knights who've just
gone away arrived. Which is: whether you know what other rewards
— apart from those we've already talked about that he granted to
those four knights — the count of Barcelona conferred in the course
of the Tortosa campaign. As the siege was so long and bitter, I expect
lots of people must have suffered a great deal.
LIVIO: Whether he granted other rewards? That magnanimous prince
granted so many that he kept nothing for himself.
DON PEDRO: Really?
LIVIO: It's exactly as I say, because, first of all, he gave the Genoese a
third of the whole city, and, as I've already told you, he gave another
third to Montcada, and he gave the last third to the knights Templar,
who also joined him on the campaign. The only person he didn't
reward was one of the barons who took part in the conquest, Mossèn
Guillem, lord of Montpellier, because he said he didn't want anything, and that he'd only gone there to give support to the count,
who was a relative of his. That's why the count decided to commem-

orate and celebrate Mossèn Guillem by establishing in Tortosa the system of weights and measures used in Montpellier, as is still the case today. The count also gave his servant Berenguer Pinyol the village of Costumà; he gave Bernat Bell-lloc the fief of Aldea, near Amposta; he gave his chamberlain, Guillem Sunyer, the castle of Camarles; to Copons he gave Godall; and to many other minor noblemen and patricians he made gifts of other places that are still important today within the jurisdiction of Tortosa. Finally, to the patricians of Barcelona, for the excellent way they'd served him on the campaign, he granted the privilege of wearing gold chains and gold swords and spurs, and fighting on horseback and having to be issued with a challenge before a duel, just as is the case with knights.

Don Pedro: Let's say no more. At that time men were quite right to do all they were capable of, as they lost nothing by their efforts in terms of honour and profit, and princes acted out of good sense rather than sentiment, whereas nowadays — unless you're the king's favourite or the favourite's best friend — you can carry out greater feats than Caesar and they just don't give a damn.

Fabio: Why did the Genoese take part? Were they paid, or was it more a question of friendship?

Livio: The count's chronicle says they were paid, but the Genoese chronicle says it was out of friendship and in the service of God. Actually, I'd prefer to believe the Genoese version, because the fact is that, when the city had been won, the count (as I've already said) gave them one third of it, which, a couple of years later, they sold back to him, only holding onto some exemptions from taxation that they enjoyed then, and indeed still do. If he'd paid them, there wouldn't have been any reason to give them a third of the city — and what a city!

Don Pedro: I rather like your reasoning. If he'd wanted to reward them out of courtesy, the recompense would have had to be something other than the estate that had been conquered. So the count really did keep nothing for himself, then? ·

Livio: Not as far as property is concerned. What he wanted was loyalty. He wanted to be recognised as sovereign lord, and he wanted to be able to appoint the sheriff himself, just as the king does today in order to execute whatever provisions are determined by the city officials. But the sheriff is so restricted in his office that, if he only does what he's entitled to do, as I've said, he has hardly anything to do other than carry out what's been decided by the officers who deal with criminal and civil cases, and the others who have charge of the city administration, as Fabio here knows better than I do.

FABIO: That's correct. And, as far as jurisdiction goes, it's barely credible how much the citizens were given. In fact, it's so much that, even when the king actually resides in Tortosa, it's the city officers who administer justice, not the officers of the royal court.

DON PEDRO: Is that really possible?

FABIO: That's what happens and, if you really want to know, I'll tell you the precise formula that goes to prove it.

DON PEDRO: I'd be very pleased to hear you explain that. It would be a good idea if you told us, otherwise we might think badly of you and wonder whether it was just love of your land that made you speak at such length. The fact is it's quite unheard of. After all, not even the Aragonese enjoy a privilege like that, since in Aragon in certain cases it's the king and his officers who carry out justice, and you say that here it's only the city officers who do. I beg you not to think us, or at least me, so naive or so easy to convince about such outlandish notions. That's why, as I say, you need to give better proof regarding this matter than regarding all the others we've been discussing, because this is harder to believe than any of them.

FABIO: I tell you again: it happened just as I've explained. The formal declaration that proves it is this, and you'll find it in a legal ruling in Latin made by Mossèn Grau de Palou in respect of the jurisdiction of the king and the city which is kept in the city offices:

In all other cases, be they criminal or civil, both in principal actions and in appeals, whether they concern pure and mixed authority or jurisdiction, that are presented either in the city of Tortosa or within its bounds, I pronounce and declare that the entire competence and submission pertain exclusively to the local corporation and the foremost men of the city of Tortosa, in the presence of the sheriff or his deputy, without the king, the queen, the duke or any of their representatives — be they present or absent from the said city and its bounds and territory — in any way being empowered to intervene in these matters.[43]

And the sentence goes on insisting on the issue at great length, though the words I've just quoted are the key ones. What do you say to that, then, Don Pedro? Are you satisfied?

43 In the original, this is quoted in Latin.

DON PEDRO: All I can say is that I'm quite amazed by what I've heard, and I'd very much like to know why the count granted such very broad jurisdiction. It's really quite bizarre, and utterly unlike anything I've ever heard of. It's perfectly true that the Aragonese — as it was they who reconquered the kingdom from the Moors — chose their king and agreed their code of law and placed the chief justice of Aragon between themselves and the king and endowed him with all the jurisdiction, pre-eminence and authority that we're all aware of. But I know that the citizens here didn't conquer the city themselves — it was the count, the Genoese, the Templars, the lord of Montpellier, Montcada and, when all's said and done, all the other Catalans, who won it. I'd just like to be able to get to the bottom of this and get it clear. That would really make me happy!

FABIO: Livio will be able to explain it better than me, as he knows more about it. I know about the effects, but not the causes.

LIVIO: I'll explain, but first, Don Pedro, I think you should understand that that jurisdiction has become more ineffectual than it ought to have done.

DON PEDRO: I too would like to think that people who live under the rule of a king can't carry on forever enjoying that much freedom.

LIVIO: That's very true, because princes are never short of means to bring their subjects under their control. As I say, I don't know which of the counts of Barcelona it was who managed to do that here. Seeing that the powers he had in Catalonia were very limited, that count persuaded the Catalans to agree the royal prerogatives that are enjoyed today by the king. Since then, they've never been able to turn the clock back and enjoy the rights they'd acquired by their own efforts. Which is why Miquel Terçà — a native of this city, the Catalan head of the Supreme Royal Council of the Crown of Aragon and, as you know, a man of the most singular intelligence and learning — once, when he was in the administrative offices here dealing with business to do with royal property, said, and said very well, in regard to the matter in hand: "Look, sirs, don't you touch anything that belongs to the king, but at the same time I advise you not to give him anything that's yours, because *he* wouldn't miss it, but *you* might well do."

FABIO: That was the advice of a truly good friend and a good citizen. It looks to me as though what happened to the canons here a long time ago is what also happened to the Catalans: as the bishops didn't derive enough income from their dioceses, the canons gave them some of theirs, and now the bishops are wealthy, whilst the canons live in misery and sorely regret having been so generous.

LIVIO: That's right. And that's where the saying comes from that goes: "If you don't look ahead, you'll fall over backwards." But let's get back to what we were talking about. What I say, Don Pedro, is that, as far as things to do with the privileges and freedoms of Tortosa are concerned, there are so many of them and they're so marvellous, both in general terms and in particular, that they're hard to credit and need plenty of time to expound, and nobody will believe you unless you spell out all the details. However, as I'm speaking here in the city itself, and the evidence is here before our very eyes, I won't hesitate to tell you everything I've read and heard about it.

What you need to understand is that, besides what Fabio has already said about its jurisdiction, Tortosa has also got amazing privileges that were obtained later on in return for services rendered and which are no less remarkable than its jurisdiction. First of all, the city isn't bound to contribute to the army or the cavalry, and the usage known as *Princeps namque*[44] doesn't apply, nor does the requirement to provide a local militia, or a thousand less important things that vassals are usually bound to supply to their kings and lords.

But, as regards the reason for the great freedom and the broad jurisdiction that so amaze you, Don Pedro, this is how it came about. A few months after the count of Barcelona had won Tortosa and La Suda, he left to go and conquer the city of Lleida. And, even though things went well for him there, in the middle of it all he still had to cope with a lot of troubles and difficulties. Well, while he was in the midst of that predicament, the relief force that the Moors of Tortosa were expecting, as I said earlier, even though it was too late for it to save and restore the city to them, was eager to reach the city and try to win it back, which is why they laid the cruellest and severest siege that's ever been seen against a town, because they brought together all the Moors of Valencia, Murcia, Aragon and Catalonia, where there were still plenty of them. And, even though the circumference of the city is great, as you can see, they managed to surround it completely, and

---

44 *Princeps namque* is the name of a *usatge*, or law of Barcelona, dating from the 11th century, which regulated the defence of the prince and the principality of Catalonia and the organisation of its military forces.

they set up part of their camp by the river, because, with Tortosa being located as it is, the river can always provide a relief route.

The newly installed Christian inhabitants resisted the determination and fury of the Moors as manfully as they could. But, as things became ever tighter and the Moors didn't allow the wretched city a moment's respite, the citizens decided to send to the count for help, as I told you earlier, by which time he was already in Urgell. Upon which, he replied that there was no way he could come to their aid at that moment, because he was so taken up with the conquests he was making there, and that they should therefore do the best they could, as he couldn't do anything to help.

DON PEDRO: What a harsh reply that was! It must have been very hard for them to take, given the dire straits they were in.

LIVIO: You can just imagine what it must have been like for those poor people to hear such a harsh reply from their lord, seeing that they'd put all their hopes in him. However — disappointed as they were by the count's reply, realising that they could expect little aid from elsewhere, and seeing the plight they were in — the citizens held a meeting of their Council and listened to the many different opinions that were voiced there. Since they couldn't defend themselves by their own means, and their prince and lord couldn't come to their aid, considering the ferocious threat of the enemy, and aware that the Moors would have no mercy on them because they were incensed with them on account of the ill treatment that they claimed to have received from the Christians when Tortosa was captured from them; fearing that, if they fell into the enemy's hands, they and their women and children would be treated with extreme cruelty, and that the women, the children and anyone not capable of making weapons for the Moors would be killed, and all their treasure and belongings burned, as happened in Saguntum and Numantia, they determined that they would storm out of the city in desperation and die attacking the enemy.

FABIO: What a courageous decision! What agony those poor Christians must have been suffering at that moment!

DON PEDRO: That's absolutely true, Livio!

LIVIO: There's no doubt about it. But what happened next and what was done afterwards, as regards the freedoms of the city, is testimony and proof enough of what I've been saying. When they'd all agreed about what to do, one of the men who'd been present at the Council meeting and who felt extremely upset by the decision because he loved his wife so much, went and told her what had been agreed. She became so frightened that she said to her husband: "When you go back to the meeting, don't say anything and don't let anyone know that you've told me, and I'll try to find a better way out of this awful plight than the one they've decided on."

Thinking carefully about the terrible predicament that faced them, that diligent matron quietly gathered together in a church all the other women in the city and told them everything she knew had been happening, though without letting them know where she'd heard it from, and said that it was very important that, between them all, they think up some way out of the terrible situation they were in, if they were to avoid their inevitable death and that of all their children. When the assembled women heard the awful news and realised how cruel and desperate the sentence was that threatened them and their children, they discussed the many different views that were expressed, and they resolved to approach their husbands who were at the council meeting and beg them not to carry out the terrible plan that they'd decided on, telling them it was unworthy of Christians, that almighty and merciful God would be most ill served by such lack of trust in His mercy and omnipotence, that if any other peoples in Spain had followed such a cruel and atrocious course of action they were simply faithless infidels who considered that all their happiness and glory consisted merely in worldly goods, that they shouldn't forget that they were Christians and that, although God sometimes punishes Christians for their sins, He doesn't abandon them forever. Finally, they told them that they'd thought of a much better and more sensible way out of the situation they were all in, which was that the women would all arm themselves and climb up onto the battlements with lances and other weapons, and with lots of banners and drums, and would make a great display and lots of warlike noise; and that, at the same time, the men, for their part, well armed and resolute, would attack the besieging enemy near St. John's church, which, as a result of this action, was named 'of the Camp', as it's still known today. However, before doing that, they should send out two men towards the enemy camp, as if they were sending them somewhere else, and make sure they were captured by the Moors, and they should carry letters saying that that very night a large relief force had entered the city. If they did that, the women assured them, they were convinced that God would grant them total victory.

DON PEDRO: My goodness, what a marvellous idea! It reminds me of the trick that the Greeks used in order to take Troy when they left that statue of Pallas Athena and sent in Sinon to give a false account of their plans.[45]

LIVIO: That's true, but that was in order to destroy a city, and this was in order to save one. Well, the men listened and took in the firm decision sent them by those judicious and courageous women; and, as it sounded as if it had come from God, they accepted it. And when they'd done everything that had to be done first — that is, sent the men towards the enemy camp, as had been agreed, and armed the women in the appointed manner and sent them up to the battlements — the men went out to battle with enormous fury, and they fared so well that they slaughtered an uncountable number of Moors, and the rest fled in such tremendous fear and riot that the soldiers in the other camps around the city also took flight, and not one of them stood his ground, so that the Christians won the day and took everything the Moors had left behind, which was an infinite amount.

FABIO: Holy Mary, Livio! Did that really happen? I'm absolutely delighted. I'd never heard that story.

LIVIO: I can well believe that. The people of this city have never been particularly concerned about knowing who they are or where they came from. That isn't the case with the comparable feat achieved by the women of the Catalans and the Almogavers in the city of Gallipoli, near Constantinople, in 1308, when their husbands went out to fight and beat the Genoese, because Zurita recounts that episode in his *Annals of Aragon*, vol. II, book VI, chapter 7, towards the end. In fact, our people only got to know the real name of Tortosa some twenty years ago.

DON PEDRO: I take what you've just said as almost miraculous.

LIVIO: You might well think so, and there actually is a miracle involved, if what happened with the pilgrim really occurred.

DON PEDRO: What's this about a pilgrim?

---

45 The story of Sinon appears in the *Aeneid*. A Greek soldier, Sinon, pretended to desert to the Trojans and persuaded them to take the wooden horse into their city. Don Pedro appears to mix that story up with the story of the Palladion (which also appears in the *Aeneid*), the wooden statue of Pallas Athena that was stolen from Troy and taken to Rome.

LIVIO: It was like this. When the battle was raging between the Christians and the Moors, one Moorish squadron that hadn't realised that the rest had been defeated, because it was far away from the main scene of the action, decided to launch an assault on the city whilst the rest were fighting. And, just as they were about to enter the city, a pilgrim came towards them who'd been sitting by the gate and started battling with them with such force and fury that he made them retreat and take flight. And that was just at the moment that the rest of the Moors were swept from the field.

FABIO: I've heard that story too about the pilgrim many a time, but I didn't know what battle it happened in.

LIVIO: I'm not too certain about that, either, and I'm not very sure about the details, but that's what they say happened, and that's what everybody keeps repeating and believes. And we can see with our own eyes the statue of that pilgrim by the gate where he sat when the Moors were about to enter the city, and it's said that it was placed there in memory of that miracle. And the gate is still called the Portal del Romeu, or Pilgrim's Gate.

DON PEDRO: In other words, heaven and earth came together in the conquest of the city! And what happened then?

LIVIO: When that had happened, Count Ramon Berenguer found that he was free of his other commitments and came over here to Tortosa from Lleida in order to make his excuses and apologise for not coming to their aid and for having left the people of Tortosa in the lurch in their hour of need. And, to tell you the truth, when he reached the gate, the citizens shut it firmly in his face.

DON PEDRO: What a brilliant reply, by Jove! Wasn't that amusing!

FABIO: Now I can see that our forefathers were braver than I'd imagined. We ought to be better thought of when it comes to valour and virtue.

LIVIO: I'm very pleased, Fabio, that you're beginning to see who you are and to take note of the event. If you wait a little, you'll hear still more. But I'm afraid you'll quickly forget it and, if you don't get anything from it... What are you laughing about now? If only I didn't get things right so much, I'd be really happy, and the city would acquire even more distinction than it has.

But, getting back to the point... When the count saw the citizens shutting the gate in his face, he realised they were right to do so and started flattering them with sweet words with a view to winning back their love and loyalty, telling them to remember that it was he who'd settled them in this good and pleasant land, that it had cost him dearly in hard work, fatigue and expense, that he was sorrier than anyone that he hadn't been able to come to their rescue, and assuring them that in the future he would make up for it to such an extent that they would clearly see the affection he felt for them. When the citizens heard these and other sugary words dropping from the count's mouth, they replied that actually it wasn't their wish to stop having him as their lord; in fact, they were content to place themselves under his authority and lordship. However, as he'd abandoned them in their hour of need and misfortune, and they'd had to rely entirely on their own strength and native wit to overcome the danger and the total ruin that had threatened them, which was as if they'd conquered themselves, it seemed reasonable that the count should settle them in the city in complete accordance with their wishes and grant them the privileges and freedoms that they desired. And the count gladly acceded to their petition, granting them licence to lay down as they thought best the laws and statutes that were to govern them. And, having obtained that authorisation, they approved the laws and customs that Fabio is well acquainted with, and the count confirmed them exactly in the form they wrote them out in. However, they were so broad in their terms that they went beyond any proper bounds and limits, and some of the customary laws were actually declared to be contrary to canon law and to the practice of good Christians, so that in the end they had to amend and limit and improve them.

FABIO: I couldn't tell you exactly how or why they were made the way they were, but I can tell you that there are plenty of them, and in the charter of settlement, quite apart from what we've got in the customary law and other specific privileges, they gave us so much that it's impossible to believe.[46]

LIVIO: That's how it is. But let's spell it out. As we said earlier in a different context, we can say exactly what we like amongst ourselves. Those who settled here that last time were really brave — there's no getting away from it. The works they did are proof enough. But there's one thing I think they got really wrong. In fact, I actually reckon they showed a mean spirit. Indeed, I'd almost say villainy, or maybe it was a question of envy.

---

[46] The Carta de Població, or charter of settlement, was accorded by Ramon Berenguer IV in 1149.

FABIO: And what, on your life, was that? I'm astounded that you're prepared to speak like that.

LIVIO: Don't you agree that it was a bad thing to do — a real blunder —
to demand as a privilege that no knight could take part in the city government, but that the patricians could, so long as they didn't actually become knights and take part in chivalric pursuits?[47]

DON PEDRO: You're joking!

LIVIO: Not a bit of it.

DON PEDRO: So what kind of activities were they supposed to perform?
Peasant ones?

LIVIO: That's what it looked like, and that's why Colonel Joan d'Aldana,
a native of the city, quipped that Tortosa had privileges that enabled
it to appoint peasants.

DON PEDRO: Aldana was absolutely right to say that, and you were all
quite wrong to preserve that kind of privilege in such an honourable
town as this.

LIVIO: We've also got a law, or a privilege, or whatever, that says that any
nobleman who's in debt can have his arms and his horse impounded.

DON PEDRO: I'll get really angry if I hear any more ridiculous things like
that! You must be joking!

LIVIO: Not at all, I assure you. It's just as I say.

DON PEDRO: How can that be, if it's against the common usages and
against the privileges of nobility granted to knights long before that
customary law was granted to Tortosa?

FABIO: And that isn't kept, either...

LIVIO: I think it was meant to be kept. And I don't say that because the
nobility don't pay tax on imports and exports. I say it because they
asked for too much and used their mouths as measures.

DON PEDRO: Why don't you just go and burn those impious and crazy
privileges and customary laws? All they do is kick out those people
who ought to be honoured the most. Don't you realise that, the more
noblemen there are in a city, the more distinguished it is and the
more its artisans thrive? What you've explained sounds completely
barbarous to me. Fabio, as you're involved in the administration, I
urge you to try and get such an unpleasant and unreasonable a thing
as that sorted out. Being as fond of this town as I am, as I've told you,

47 This appears to have been a matter that personally exercised Cristòfol Despuig. He
never took steps to become a knight, probably because that would have prevented him
from taking office in the Tortosa municipal council.

I'm really sorry that that should be happening. In Valencia, Barcelona and other similar cities, knights can be involved in municipal government. In Lleida, they don't just allow them to join: it's actually laid down that no-one can become chief justice — what they call the *Paer* and what you call the *Procurador* — unless he's a knight, and they actually prefer him to be a lord of vassals. Just see how different that is from what you do here! Prudence ought to teach you to follow the example of the best practice around you.

LIVIO: Oh! How many times have I preached that myself and banged my head against a brick wall! I've never been believed, or even listened to! The ridiculous thing is that every one of those gentlemen is against those privileges when you speak to him on his own and says they ought to be done away with, but when they're gathered together they do nothing to remedy the situation.

DON PEDRO: In that case, I expect there can't have been many noblemen left at the conquest, if they constrained them that much.

FABIO: I don't know if there were only a few then, but there are certainly only a few now.

LIVIO: To tell you the truth, there were never very many, but there were more than there are now, if you go back far enough. But the whole thing declined to such an extent that there were only two or three noble families left in the city. After a time they increased, and now there are more. There are a lot of them, both because some knights have come to settle here from elsewhere and because some patricians here have become knights.

DON PEDRO: I'm pleased to hear that they realise what's what. You'd have to be blind to want to belong to the commons, instead of moving up to the noble estate, seeing how they're men of such ability and, indeed, most honourable, because they're as different as black is from white as regards honour and distinction. The proof is perfectly obvious. The king is a knight, as are all the rulers in the world, and the noble estate enjoys great exemptions that the commons don't.

FABIO: That is indeed so, but noblemen are bound to go about more showily than the rest, whereas ordinary citizens can live a lot more unconstrained. And, as the saying goes, changing your habits is like dying. That's the reason why we want to stay the same, and also because patricians are held in the same high esteem here as in Barcelona. That being so, it looks as though we can be happy enough in the estate we're in.

LIVIO: I admit that the patricians here are most honourable and, as has already been said, they enjoy plenty of authority. But, if you wanted to achieve the status of what they call "honourable citizens" in Barcelona, you'd have to register, as they do,[48] and have the privileges that they have, otherwise your estate would be bound to be less than perfect and to suffer serious difficulties, which I won't go into so that you don't see me prove the saying, "Telling the truth loses you friends." However, as I'm speaking amongst judicious people, I think you get the idea. I'll just say this for your benefit: in Barcelona they don't admit a man because he's rich, if he lacks other qualities that are required for a particular estate. And that's why they prefer a man who's been named an honourable citizen in Barcelona to a man who's been knighted by the king if he doesn't possess the necessary qualities and distinction.

DON PEDRO: It's been a pleasure to hear the pros and cons regarding all of that. I'm really very pleased. But, Fabio, I go back to the business of your not being keen to be knighted because of all the ceremonies involved and then having to go around dressed more showily. As the place isn't very big, I reckon you aren't particularly bothered about the way you live. At least, it looks to me as though you all dress the same. Don't tell me it's just a question of "My father's a Moor, so I'm a Moor, too."

LIVIO: Don Pedro is quite correct, although there are also other fetters that keep those gentlemen tied hand and foot and prevent them breaking free from their circle or kicking off their clogs.

DON PEDRO: What, for heaven's sake?

LIVIO: The treasure chest of the Diputació[49] of Catalonia, and the profit they've seen some men from here obtain who've been involved in administrating it. The fact is, it's the idol that all men adore with great devotion. That's what, in the last resort, prevents them becoming knights. The business about the city isn't the real problem, and it would be easy to resolve, if only they wanted to.

FABIO: You've hit the nail on the head. That's what it's about, nothing else, if the truth is to be told. If they knighted us, there's no doubt that we'd lose that place.

---

[48] The *ciutadans honrats* formed part of the oligarchic patriciate of Barcelona. In 1510, 130 people were registered as such. Livio goes on to suggest that what counts in Tortosa, in order to become a *ciutadà honrat*, is money, rather than noble qualities

[49] The Diputació was the Standing Commission of the Parliamentary Estates, whose leaders or officers were known as Diputats.

DON PEDRO: What? Aren't noblemen allowed to be involved in the government of the Diputació? They are in Valencia.

LIVIO: You really are amusing! They do indeed go into government, but the fact is this, and, as we're talking about it, I shan't hesitate to spell it out. In the olden days, as you must know, the representatives were elected, that's to say chosen by oral votes. And, as some Catalan lords had the power to control the voters' freedom, so that only the representatives they wanted got elected, it was decided that, in order to solve that problem, all three estates be registered — that is the ecclesiastical estate, the nobility and the commons — and that a certain number of men be chosen from each estate in the different jurisdictional districts of Catalonia, and that the members and auditors be chosen from amongst them, as still happens today. And, in order to carry out that procedure, it was necessary to bring all the estates together. Unfortunately for the noble estate of this district, none of the nobility was present at the meeting, and one Joan Jordà — Guillem Ramon Jordà's father — was sent by the commons. In the district of Tortosa twenty-four places were allotted to the nobles and the commons: that is, twelve members and twelve auditors. When Jordà realised that there was no nobleman there who could stand in his way or go against him, he didn't hesitate to demand all the twenty-four places for the commons, saying there were no noblemen in the district. And, as there was no-one there to contradict him, he had no trouble being allotted all those places for the commons. All, that is, except for one place that was demanded by someone who asked for it for a relative by the name of Montrós who, he said, was resident here, and it was allotted to him. So the commons got twenty-three, and the local nobility were left out completely. That's the answer to your question.

DON PEDRO: By Jesus! I'm horrified by that. That was a bigger blunder than what they did in relation to customary law.

LIVIO: Yes, Holy Mary! Then they only took what was theirs, as they'd won it by risking and endangering their own blood. But this was robbery by lies, as there were as many noblemen as commons representatives in Tortosa and its district — you have to take the whole district into account — and maybe more, as not all those who call themselves patricians count as such for a position like that. And it follows that, if there aren't that many, some unqualified patricians must be placed in the lottery for office, and that's a serious defect in such a proper

government. Jordà ought to have thought carefully about that, for
the sake of his own honour and his fellows', assuming he didn't care
to respect the municipal government's honoured and undisputed
authority or the integrity of his own conscience. But, God willing,
time will come when this will be put right.

FABIO: Livio, I don't see that there are as many noble houses as that in
Tortosa and its district. At least, I don't think there were then.

LIVIO: Even then there were plenty.

FABIO: And which were they, by your life, as I just don't remember?

LIVIO: There were the Pinyols, the Icarts, the Garidells, the
Montroses, the Abellas, the Proençals, the Canaders and the
Despuigs. That's as far as the city goes. In the Tortosa district there
were the Ciscars in Horta, the Lioris in Gandesa, the Herèdias in
Ulldecona, and the Guiots. Then the other Herèdias in Batea, the
Castellbells in Flix, the Vilanovas also in Flix, and the Socarrats in
Ascó. Those, Fabio, were the ones that were there already, so you
can understand and consider just how manifest Jordà's calumny
was, because, were I to try to remember all the ones that are there
now, it would be a lot more than the ones I've just named, because,
as you know, a lot became knights, both in the city and in its district,
and, as I said earlier, others came and settled here who were per-
sons of quality. And the fact is that there aren't as many as eighteen
heads amongst the commons who deserve a place on the Diputació, and, as I said, there are twenty-three of them, whereas the
nobles, of whom there are so many, have only got one. Just look and
see if the matter isn't perfectly clear.

DON PEDRO: Fabio, please don't answer him. There's nothing more to
be said. Let's just put an end to the discussion.

FABIO: I shan't say another thing, except just that the nobles have got
two places now, because a few years back Nofre de Liori got another
one added.

DON PEDRO: And who was it given to?

FABIO: Liori got it himself.

DON PEDRO: Just like that grocer in Tarragona.[50]

LIVIO: It was right that he got it, as he'd obtained it by his tenacity and
litigation, which wasn't to be sneezed at.

---

[50] The reference is to a legendary grocer who borrowed things and did not give them
back.

DON PEDRO: I'd say it would be a good idea if the nobles did their best to get a couple more places as auditors of the accounts: then the matter would be put right or, at least, patched up.

LIVIO: I at least want to do what I can in that respect at the next meeting of the assembly.

DON PEDRO: Tell me. Is this Dona Joana's house?

LIVIO: Yes, it is.

DON PEDRO: I bring her greetings from a lady who's a great friend — maybe even a relative — of hers. As we're here, please, let's go and give her those greetings, and I'll have got that over and done with, and we'll be able to enjoy some good conversation and a pleasant sight, as she's a very elegant and refined lady, and I'm most devoted to her, and then we can get back to our conversation.

LIVIO: We'll do whatever you say.

FABIO: Let's go. We've got plenty of time for everything.

The Fourth Dialogue

THE FOURTH DIALOGUE, WHICH TREATS OF THE
FOUNDATION AND THE NAME OF TORTOSA, AND IN WHICH
A CERTAIN BADGE IS RECALLED THAT THE WOMEN OF THE
CITY WORE IN OLDEN TIMES BECAUSE OF A FEAT THAT THEY
PERFORMED FOR THE CITY'S BENEFIT SHORTLY AFTER
THE CONQUEST. THE SPEAKERS ARE THE SAME.

Speakers:
DON PEDRO, a Valencian; FABIO, a gentleman;
LIVIO, a knight.

DON PEDRO: Livio, before we get involved in any other topics, you must give me the pleasure of telling me — because I'm really keen to know — what reward or honour did the citizens of Tortosa grant to those valorous women for the superb feat and the salutary counsel that brought about such a triumph. The fact is I've never heard or read of anything more remarkable, and I'm amazed that it's just been buried and consigned to oblivion. The counsel and the decision taken by the inhabitants of Saguntum and Numantia, which were comparable to those taken by the people of Tortosa, are so famous throughout the world that there's no-one who hasn't heard of them, and *they* led to the direst consequences. So why should the citizens of Tortosa, who brought about a glorious outcome that redounded to the honour of the name of Jesus Christ and the benefit of the people, be so shrouded in silence and disregard? That's really a great misfortune! It's an enormous omission! A universal suppression! I just can't get over it!

LIVIO: It's perfectly natural and normal for people to remember bad things more than good ones, and the reason is that, as the philosophers say, since nature is more inclined towards evil than good, it also retains the memory of bad things better than good ones, because evil is more agreeable to it. None the less, it goes without saying that it's a great misfortune that something as singular and important as that should have been buried like this. But, do you know why I think that came about? Because men have always fallen short when it comes to writing in praise of women; and they, poor things, as they lack education, can't do it for themselves. That's why their good works and their virtues remain forgotten and unknown. But, as truth is the daughter of time, time itself, despite men's unconcern, gives birth to truth in its own time, as is the case now, because this conversation will enable you to understand and then make known what in actual fact happened regarding what I've been telling you. And, as for what you want to know — namely, what honour and reward was granted to those brave and prudent women for such a heroic deed — I can tell you that it was so meagre that it was hardly anything at all, compared to what it ought to have been. However, I reckon it was due to the stinginess of the men — they must have realised the merit of that extraordinary act. But it must have been forgotten about, thanks to those honourable matrons' great moderation, since it may well be thought that, as they were so well endowed with the virtue of fortitude, they wouldn't be lacking in the virtue of temperance, because those two virtues usually go hand in hand.

What was done, or at least what I've found out, is that, first of all, in order to preserve the memory of that feat, the men directed that all the women should wear over their clothes a crimson or scarlet battleaxe on a short cloak like a Carthusian friar's scapulary that they called a 'pastime' and that looked like the surcoat that soldiers wear over their armour. Later they ordered that, whenever a young man went to his fiancée's house to take her to mass, as is common custom, the women who accompanied him, who are always many, should walk ahead of all the men, even if officers of the king or the city were present.

FABIO: I've seen that done, and quite recently.

LIVIO: So have I. In addition, they ordered that women shouldn't pay taxes on their bonnets or any kind of headgear, and that, if they outlived their husbands, they should inherit all and every kind of dress and jewelry that their husbands had given them, however expensive they might be. That's what was done for them. I've also heard say — though I'm not as sure about this as I ought to be — that they laid

down that, at the wedding mass, the bride should sit on the right, but
that the cathedral curates put an end to that practice because they
didn't know the reason why it was instituted and thought it was a
mark of bad practice and bad manners, rather than pre-eminence.

DON PEDRO: All that was fine, but the bit about the battleaxes must have
been quite amusing. How funny the women must have looked wearing that odd emblem! They must have looked like the nuns of
Jonqueres in Barcelona![51] I can tell you it was a very bad idea to allow
such an unusual practice to fall into disuse. When did that happen?

LIVIO: It can't have been all that long ago, because I've heard the
Reverend Baltasar Sorió — who, as you know, is a lector in the cathedral and a person of great authority and learning, over ninety years
old now — say that he's seen plenty of those garments which, as I say,
they called 'pastimes', with the scarlet battleaxe badge, and he says
he saw one in Archdeacon Garret's house for several years after he
first arrived in Tortosa, although they were no longer being worn
when he saw them, but their use couldn't have been abandoned very
long before that, as they could still be found in ladies' houses. And
I've heard Francina Despuig — Pere Joan Despuig's wife and, as you
know, a grand lady who possessed great authority, was known for
speaking the truth and was a worthy successor to those distinguished
women[52] — tell how, when she was very young, you could still find lots
of those garments with the battleaxe badges in Tortosa, and there was
hardly a single honourable woman who didn't possess one, although
even then they were no longer actually worn. And I've heard the
same from nearly all the elderly people I've known.

DON PEDRO: A thing like that ought never to have been allowed to dis-
appear!

FABIO: It wouldn't be a bad idea to restore it, and to allow the women
to walk ahead of the men.

DON PEDRO: I don't think I'd allow anything to do with preserving the
memory of such a singular feat to be lost, especially the part to do
with the battleaxes!

FABIO: I reckon it would be impossible, or at least very difficult, to get
them restored and brought back into such general use as before, but

---

[51] The nuns, who had moved from Sabadell to the convent in Barcelona, in Jonqueres
Street, at the end of the 13th century, enjoyed many unusual privileges, including the right
to wear elegant clothes.
[52] Pere Joan Despuig and Francina Savartès were the author's parents.

the following could be done, and it would be a happy compromise between the two extremes: the wives of the three city representatives could wear those badges, as well as the wives of the mayor and the chief magistrate, because, as they represent the jurisdiction and estate of the whole city, those five ladies — their wives — would represent the memory of that singular deed, thanks to which their husbands have been enabled to discharge those offices.

LIVIO: It would be better if the wives of all the officers wore them, as all of them are involved in the administration.

FABIO: That's a good idea, too. I've got nothing against it.

DON PEDRO: And it would be like what Gonçalo Hernández said after winning the battle of Cerignola. Wishing to honour two knights who'd served him very well in battle, he turned to those who were eating with him and said: "Let those two knights come and sit down to eat, for, if it weren't for them, we wouldn't be eating anything."

LIVIO: Let's hope God inspires the heart and the will of those who're in charge of the government and makes them think more carefully and seriously than they've done up to now about this matter and about all those many others that have to do with the enhancement and administration of this town. I've badgered them a thousand times to get rid of all those eaves, as they're ugly and unhealthy, and to clear up the litter. There's so much, and they've got perfectly good and efficient ways of doing it. I keep on telling them that, since the city is splendidly graced with all kinds of natural elements, it's the councillors' fault if artificial adornments are missing, but they never listen to me.

FABIO: Bit by bit, it will all be put right. It will all be done in good time. As you can see, the city is being improved and enlarged in a thousand ways, especially in its public buildings and private houses. And the people's behaviour is improving, too. In fact, it's all a lot better than it was twenty-five years ago. Just look what's been done in the cathedral. Look how stylish, beautiful and splendid it is! Look what magnificent buildings the Royal Colleges are that are going up in St. Dominic's — one for the education of the sons of new Christians converted from Islam, the other for teaching theology and other subjects. Look at the improvements that have been made to houses, both outside and inside the city, and how many splendid mansions have been built from scratch, and how many studies or mezzanines there are in them, and how well furnished they are, and how many more tapestries there are in Tortosa today than there used to be, and what bed linen and silverware! You can see for yourselves that all of this is far better than it used to be. Look, too, at the abutment of the bridge that we've got right in front of us. It's a handsome and a practical structure, and it's made it possible to improve the way the bridge is cleverly supported by those ten boats. It's definitely a lot better than it was. And the boats won't get old so quickly as when there were eleven of them. That's just one of the many improvements that this excellent work has made possible.[53]

DON PEDRO: Certainly, it's very timely, and whoever was responsible for it deserves praise. I recall I don't remember what obstruction exactly used to be caused by an ugly bulwark that used to be here. It was just like a pauper's hovel. And at the abutment, I remember, there used to be props, with a lump on top, like on the bridge at Fraga or Sant Boi.

FABIO: That's right. And look at the way the population has grown. It's nearly a third larger than it was twenty-five years ago. Look how polished the citizens are, and how much better groomed, and how much more courteously they treat one another than they used to, and how much the ladies have improved their deportment and their dress. We've seen all those things a lot worse than they are now. Ladies are so elegant nowadays and wear such long skirts that you'd think they're dressed up for carnival. They really need shortening!

LIVIO: My goodness, Fabio, I like the way you ended up with that bit about carnival! I'm bound to go along with everything else you say and to think as you do. After all, if we all help each other, everything will get better, which is as it should be and befits people of our quality.

DON PEDRO: Don't doubt that for a moment, for, in truth, I've witnessed the improvements that Fabio has been describing. And, if all the patricians here send their sons away to be educated, there isn't a shadow of a doubt that every day the town will improve in terms of elegance and nobility.

FABIO: We're already doing that. Nearly all of them go away to study, and we can see for sure that those who do so are at a great advantage.

LIVIO: Yes, they do go away, but, at the places where most of them are sent, they won't learn what Don Pedro is aiming at and has in mind.

53 Despuig was a member of the municipal commission set up in 1548 to reconstruct the bridge, which had been destroyed in a storm.

DON PEDRO: What? Where do you send them?

FABIO: To merchants' houses in Barcelona or Valencia, so they can learn business.

DON PEDRO: Merchants' houses? Now I'm no longer surprised that you're so careful about looking after your trademarks, as Livio was saying earlier! All I can say is I don't like what you're doing.

FABIO: Don't you like the art of business, then? I don't see how you can say that, if I heard you praising it just a couple of hours ago.

DON PEDRO: I don't dislike the art of business, but I don't agree with knights or patricians making it their main occupation. By sending your sons away to be taught by merchants, you make it clear that that's your intention. What they'll learn there isn't to open their eyes and their ears to the preservation and increase of honour, but to close them and wall them up for the benefit and increase of their pockets. That's why people talk about 'merchants' ears', because, as you know, they always keep them closed and prefer leaving honour behind in order to get on in business, even though there are those, and I know plenty of them, who are so distinguished that they're as good as knights when it comes to honour and gentility.

FABIO: But how can they learn business if they aren't taught business and learn how to keep the books? You know that in this land of ours we need to know about everything. We need to be horses with two saddles. Nobody can live in the style that's required, either here or anywhere, if all he has to rely on is what he's inherited, unless it's extremely huge, and that doesn't apply to many families.

DON PEDRO: I'm just saying that that's what I think. I don't think badly of knights or patricians who go into business — I just say you don't have to work at it quite so hard. To learn to do business you don't need to be so assiduous or spend so much time at it. You've got all the talent and the energy that's required to teach your sons how to make money through business, which is all that's needed. I can assure you that you'll never be lacking enough energy or intelligence or business partners.

LIVIO: Don Pedro is quite right, and I can vouch for the fact that what he says is perfectly true. One can learn all one needs in order to do business without making such a fuss about it. As for myself, I wasn't educated in a merchant's house, but in the house of a gentleman who was as courteous and noble in his ways as any in the entire kingdom. There, together with the sons of other knights, we were always busy with soldierly exercises, such as riding on every kind of saddle, jousting with all sorts of lances, fighting with all kinds of weapon, dancing every kind of dance, reading at set times all sorts of history books and, last but not least, always practising every sort of virtue. And, when necessary, that hasn't prevented me from knowing how to keep the books in my house or from arranging my affairs as well as some men whose education has been primarily in business. And if I don't do business all the time, it's for lack of money. When I've got ready cash available, I know perfectly well how to use it.

FABIO: Talking about which, that's why Captain Francesc Valls used to say — partly in jest and partly as a criticism — that, when the leading men here in Tortosa have got money, they're merchants; and when they haven't, they're patricians.

DON PEDRO: By Jove, that's a good one! So you mean that money reduced their rank? I think business must have been the opposite then of what it is now, don't you, Fabio? There's no need to reply to that! But how could you allow a son of yours to go and serve such a low person? It just doesn't make sense. If you do that, you'll never achieve the improvements that you say you wish for in terms of noble behaviour, greatness of spirit, valour, good horsemanship, or matters of honour. You can't learn any of those things in a merchant's house. On the contrary!

LIVIO: I think that's overdoing it a bit. I don't believe the patricians here actually aspire to as much as that. That would be going right against the privilege which, as I've said, they all enjoy that bars them from taking part in knightly pursuits.

FABIO: Livio, on that score, be a little more careful, please, so you don't sound so cruel.

LIVIO: Fabio, you can't call a father cruel if he punishes or scolds his son in order to make him live virtuously, as that very famous poet and orator Petrarch marvellously wrote in his *Triumph of Death*. And, as our Catalan saying has it: "He who loves you will chastise you." It's because I appreciate you that I warn you about what can happen to anyone who doesn't comply, at least as I see it. Beware of bad conduct, and put an end to evil ways and improper laws, for you know how that other saying goes: "Good profit from bad practice: it's best to go without it."

DON PEDRO: I think that's right. Livio's saying what he says because he holds you in esteem and wishes the best for you. But let's change the subject, Livio. What's the epigram that's carved on this jasper plaque? Is it very old? The jasper looks good to me. Does it come from far away?

LIVIO: The epigram's modern. It hasn't been there for more than nine years. It refers to the construction of the abutment of this bridge, and it contains the names of the city representatives — what you in Valencia call *Jurats*— who ordered the work to be carried out. As for the jasper, it comes from hereabouts. We've got as much as you like, and it's of superb quality. They used it for the columns in the court-yard of the Diputació palace in Barcelona.

DON PEDRO: Why don't they make whole buildings out of it?

LIVIO: Because it's very expensive to quarry. This is what the epigram says:

> *Anno a Christo nato MDXXXX*
> *VIII. Ab urbe Dertosae capta mauris*
> *debel. CCCC Carlo V. Ro. Imp. Hisp.*
> *rege. Christopho Depodio,*
> *Anton Dalmau, Mich. Xivelli*
> *Cons. ob pub. hono, decretum est*
> *hoc opus.*[54]

DON PEDRO: That name *Depodio*, in Latin... It wouldn't be the same as what later became 'Despuig,' would it?

LIVIO: That's right.

DON PEDRO: And the name *Dertosa* for this city can't be very old. I've heard it said — and I think I've read it in a translation of Livy — that the city had been called Carteja.

LIVIO: That's what some people thought, but they discovered they were wrong.

DON PEDRO: How do you mean?

LIVIO: I'll tell you. The geographers who write about Spain recall that in ancient times there was a town there called Tartesia, which in the course of time became known as Carteja, and then Tarifa. And, as there's no town in Spain whose name resembles Tartesia as much as Tortosa, they believed that Carteja — which, as I've said, had been known as Tartesia — must be the city known today as Tortosa. Others

---

54 I.e. "In the year of the birth of Christ 1548, four hundred years after Tortosa was cap-tured from the Moors by force of arms. To Charles V, Holy Roman Emperor, King of Spain, by Cristòfol Despuig, Antoni Dalmau, Miquel Xivelli, consuls, this work is carried out in honour of the people."

held that it was called Turtula, after some people in Spain who were known as the Turtulos or Turidetanos. One writer has insisted that it was called Tulcis, and that's Pere Miquel Carbonell, and he bases that on what Pomponius Mela wrote when he described the Spanish coastline, but he didn't know how to Hispanicise the word, so, instead of saying Tulcis, he says Tulas, and he didn't understand what Pomponius was referring to, as *he* didn't confuse Tulcis with Tortosa, and Tulcis isn't the name of a city, but a river, as is obvious from what Pomponius himself writes, as Calepinus asserts in his dictionary of proper names. Pomponius' exact words are these: *"Tarraco urbs est in his oris maritimarum opulentissima. Tulcis eam modicus amnis super, ingens Iberus deorsum atingit."*[55] Just tell me, for goodness' sake, how can anyone take those words to mean that Tulcis is Tortosa, or any other town, for that matter? It's a river, and it's probably the one we know today as the Francolí, which flows out to sea near Tarragona. Some people have been bold enough to state that the adverb *"deorsum"* (further down) ought to be *Dertosam*, and it's true that the clause would read better that way, and the description would be more exact. However, whatever the case, Tulcis can never be a town, but *"modicus amnis"* (the small river), as the writer says. Carbonell paid as little attention to that as to other things written about Catalonia, so that, instead of throwing light, he's left us in the dark, creating schisms and discord amongst Catalans regarding Catalonia's earliest institutions.

For the rest, it's a fact that Tortosa never had any other name but Dertosa. That's proved by what we find written — not just in the works of serious authors, both ancient and modern — but also by what we find carved in stone and metal, the most durable materials in the world. First, there's Pliny, in Book III, chapter 3, of his *Natural History*, where he describes the provinces and cities: "Forty-four peoples are subject to the jurisdiction of Tarragona, the best known amongst them, with Roman rights, being the Dertosans, the Bigargitans, the Ceritans, etc."[56] Admittedly, in other works of his, Pliny says *dertusani*, not *dertosani*, but I don't know whether it's the printers who mistakenly put in a *u* instead of an *o*. Strabo, who was an excellent geographer, says, in Book III: "At the very crossing of the

---

55 I.e. "Tarraco is the richest city on the coast, and it is watered by the small river Tulcis, beyond which lies the huge Ebro, which flows further down."
56 In the original, the quotation is cited in Latin.

Ebro is the colony of Dertosa."[57] You see: he says it was a Roman colony, and he calls it Dertosa. Ptolemy, a most ancient cosmographer, in the table referring to Europe in Book II, chapter 6, of his *Geography*, calls it Lertosa, changing the letter *D* into an *L*, maybe also as the result of a copying error, or making the mistake because he was writing so long before. Calepinus, in his dictionary of proper names, puts "*Dertosa urbs Hispaniae*" and rules out the name Lertosa that Ptolemy uses. Lucius Marineus, in his life of Count Ramon Berenguer of Barcelona, says: "Seeing that the following year, with the help of the nobles of the principality of Barcelona, he blockaded the city of Tortosa, which the Moors had seized again."[58] Florián de Ocampo — a modern, painstaking writer on a wide range of subjects and a great chronicler of Spanish history — also says its name was Dertosa. That's what you find in all those excellent and trustworthy writers. There's also an epigram carved in a jasper plaque that's ten spans long, and five wide, that was found here in the cathedral when they were digging the foundations, just over thirty years ago, for the chapel of Archdeacon Garret. It was a dozen spans below ground level, and the epigram says this:

> *P. Val Dionisio. VI. vir. aug. cui ord.*
> *Dertosai ob merita eius edi honores*
> *Decrevit. P. Val. Pardus lib. VI. vir. aug.*
> *patrono optimo.*[59]

As you can see perfectly well, it calls it *Dertosai*, which is the old genitive form. Then there are some medals that were also found here and which are so old that it's impossible to tell when they were made. They've been seen and read by lots of people in this town in recent times, and they've got the name Dertosa stamped on them. So, from everything I've said, it's obvious that this city was called Dertosa, and not Carteja or Turtula or Tulcis, as some people have thought.

DON PEDRO: You've demonstrated that so beautifully that there's no point going on having any doubts or wasting any more time on it.

FABIO: It's a bitter business, not discovering the real truth about this until now. I recall reading in the charter of settlement of Tortosa,

---

57 In the original, the quotation is cited in Latin.
58 This is cited in Latin in the original
59 I. e. "Publius Valerius Pardus, sixth *vir augustal*, dedicated it to the great patron Publius Valerius Dionisius, sixth *vir augustal*, to whom the authorities of Dertosa granted the honours of *aedile*."

drawn up by Count Ramon Berenguer and written in Latin, that he calls it *Tortosam*. It looks as if they didn't know its Latin name.

LIVIO: That's quite true. Not even notarial deeds give the name properly — instead of writing *Dertosa*, they give *Dertusa*. Didn't I say that truth is the daughter of time? Well, you can see here too that, when its time came, time gave birth to it. The same thing happened with the name of Barcelona. Until not very long ago people believed that fable about the ninth barque, or boat, of Hercules that was supposed to have given the form *Barcanona*, or *Barcinona*, whereas today we understand and take it to be a fact that the name Barcinona came from a Carthaginian general who founded it and whose name was Barcino, a member of the house and lineage from which Hannibal came. And some people say it was actually Hamilcar Barca, Hannibal's father.

DON PEDRO: I like everything you've been saying. But the thing that convinces me most is what's written on that jasper plaque and on those medals, because it seems obvious that they give the name the way it was at the time, whereas the writers could easily get it wrong, as they wrote at a distance and a lot later. As I'm a great collector of those antique medals and of epigrams like that, I'd be very pleased if you could let me have some of the ones you've got, and a copy of that epigram, and of others, if there are any more.

LIVIO: Regarding medals with the name Dertosa on them, I can't let you have any, because unfortunately only two have been found, and I want to try and get them from the person who owns them and donate them to the city's elected representatives so that they can be kept safely, as they deserve to be, in the city offices. But I can get hold of other really old medals dating back to various times and generals, because there are some very good ones to be had, most of them found right here, in silver and in other metals. In particular, I can tell you that, not eighteen years ago, when they were digging in Captain Francesc Joan Valls' house underneath his study, in order to build some stables, together with the earth they brought out lots of chunks of what looked like the iron slag that smiths get out of their forges, and, as they didn't know what it was, they threw it out into the Ebro with the earth. Well, one day when some children were playing there, they broke open some of the chunks that had remained on the river bank, and out came a whole lot of medals of the finest silver, out of which a certain person made a jug, because it was so pure. The medals were of various designs. Some had, embossed on one side, the two sons of Brutus, the one who threw the kings out of Rome, with two executioners behind them with raised axes, and on the other side a head with the inscription "Brutus" underneath.[60] I reckon those must have been amongst the earliest medals that the Romans made in silver. There were also others that had an elephant on one side, and underneath an inscription that said "Caesar," and on the other side lots of instruments to do with the augurs. And then there were others that had a bier and the inscription "*Feretrum romanorum*" on one side, and on the other side the inscription "*Silla et Rufus.*"[61] And there were also other designs that I've forgotten.

However, I'll make you a copy of that epigram, and of many of the other excellent ones that can be found around here, and I'll let you have them in a notebook, along with drawings of the medals, just as they appear. As for epigrams, I can tell you that new ones are being discovered every day. In particular, four or five years ago, when they were starting to dig the foundations for an aisle that's being built in the cathedral, they found some large slabs of stone with excellent epigrams on them referring to Roman emperors and generals. And, when the work was continued later, in 1552, and the foundations were dug for the front of the tower that faces onto Saint Blai, they found two slabs or blocks of very large square columns of dressed stone. They're the ones that serve today as the footings for that tower, from ground level up to the first wide decorative band. There was obviously a great temple in pagan times on the site of the present cathedral, because it isn't only epigrams that are found there. Wherever they dig, they find beautiful paving stones some ten spans below ground level which must have been the floor of the temple.

DON PEDRO: I'll be most grateful if you could ask to let me have everything that's found, because, as I've said, things like that simply delight me. In other words, then, Tortosa is a very ancient town. I hadn't realised.

LIVIO: It's extremely ancient. I believe it's actually the first that was built in Spain.

DON PEDRO: That's overdoing it a bit, surely! I'm afraid it's the love you have for your home town that makes you exaggerate. I know that, if

---

[60] The sons of Lucius Junius Brutus, founder of the Roman republic, attempted to overthrow the government and restore the monarchy, so the father ordered their death to maintain the republic.

[61] Quintus Pompeius Rufus (d. 88 BC) became consul alongside the future dictator Sulla.

it really were the first that was built, some of the historians who have written about the settlement of Spain would have made some mention of it.

LIVIO: I don't swear that what I say is absolutely true, and I wouldn't force anyone to regard it as an article of faith. However, one can speculate quite reasonably that that's the case, even if there's no conclusive proof, because there's no perfect way to establish anything as ancient as that, and the best one can do is make the most of what evidence there is, and that's what studying law teaches us.

DON PEDRO: True enough, but I don't think you can possibly convince me that Tortosa was the first town built in Spain.

LIVIO: That's certainly a tough thing to say. Why shouldn't one be able to provide arguments to prove that this town was the first, just as one could to prove it was a different one? As we're talking about something as ancient as that, the difficulty of establishing proof is just the same for any town. So, unless you want to believe what some philosophers hold, namely that the world has been here forever, you're bound to agree that, once God had created the world, one town or another must have been the first. So tell me, then: why shouldn't the first town in Spain have been Tortosa, at least as easily as any other? I'm convinced that, given your good judgment and the force of my arguments, I'll be able to persuade you, if you listen carefully, that my opinion on this subject is correct.

DON PEDRO: You've got our permission to say whatever you like, just so long as we've got yours not to believe whatever we don't like!

LIVIO: So be it. We start evens. Now, just listen, please. Nearly all those who've written about the settlement of the world after the Flood, and they're infinite — Berossus, Manetho, Josephus, Master Francesc Eiximenis, Juan Rodrigo, archbishop of Toledo, Annius of Viterbo, Florián de Ocampo, St. Jerome, St. Isidore — all of them unanimously affirm that Tubal, the fifth son of Japheth, who was Noah's third son, was the first to come and settle Spain, and most of them state that the place where he first landed was on the Ebro, and that he did so with all the followers who came in his fleet, and they say he settled the banks of the river and built a notable town at its entrance. And, since Amposta is where the mouth of the river was then, as at that time the sea reached up to there and even beyond, many people have inferred that Amposta was the first town that Tubal founded in Spain. That's the opinion of Master Francesc Eiximenis and of the compilers of the Catalan chronicles, and others. And, even though they're right about Tubal's arrival in that area and his founding the town at the river mouth, I don't think they're right about it being Amposta. The reason is that the writers say the first town founded by Tubal was big, and it must have been big in order to cater for the many followers that Tubal brought with him, and in Amposta you can't see a single sign or trace that it was ever any bigger than it is now. Neither the land nor the site of Amposta is such that it could have appealed to Tubal or attracted him to build an important town there. What's more, Tubal was too shrewd and experienced a man to build a town so close to the sea, what with the danger of enemy invasion and the innumerable other perils that being close to the sea involves. He would have built it by the river, the right distance away so that, on the one hand, it was far enough away from danger, and on the other, near enough not to miss out on the seaborne trade that could bene- fit his companions. He would have had one foot in the sea and the other on dry land.

FABIO: But couldn't he have avoided the danger from enemies by build- ing a solid wall around the town?

LIVIO: Yes, but in those days they hadn't yet invented walls to defend themselves from their enemies. That came a lot later. So, if it's true that the first town that Tubal built was notable, as the writers say, it can't have been Amposta, for the reasons I've just stated. And, since there's no other ancient town on these banks until you get to the sea, apart from Tortosa, clearly this must be the one that Tubal built at the entrance to the Ebro. As it wasn't more than a league away from the river mouth — because, as I've said, at that time the sea came up right to this side of Amposta and reached up as far as Campredó and Carrova — it would be quite correct to say that Tortosa was at the entrance to the river. Besides, there's another very good reason for believing that what I say is right, and that is that in ancient times Tortosa's city arms were a ship in full sail, and that's what we find per- fectly clearly on those medals that I've been talking about that bear the name of Tortosa, on which a ship is depicted in full sail. And it's likely that Tortosa adopted those arms when it was being built in order to denote the journey made by its founder and initiator, Tubal, and the full sails would denote the success of that voyage. In the light of all these reasons, conjectures and hypotheses, then, I'm con- vinced that Tortosa was the first place that was settled in Spain. Of course, it's possible that Tubal also built Amposta, as a kind of guard post at the river mouth, like a watch tower, but I don't believe it could have been the first and main settlement that those scholars I've mentioned claim. Are you convinced, then? If not, you'd better look for somebody else to give you a better explanation.

DON PEDRO: I say you've explained it all so well that, from now on, I shan't doubt it as much as I did before, because what you say sounds like the most likely explanation. By my soul, this city is indebted to you for having researched all this. The citizens really owe you their gratitude, and from now on they really ought to take the advice and counsels that you give them, as you're clearly a person who has great love for them and wish to see them honoured and prosperous.

FABIO: For my part, in particular, I can tell you that I'm most obliged to you. I don't know how we can thank you for such a very special favour as the one you're offering us all.

LIVIO: I'm obliged to do that, and more, in Tortosa's honour, both because of my natural obligation, being a native of the city, and because my family has lived here ever since it was conquered. As it has pleased God that I should have come by knowledge of its affairs, it's proper that, when I've got the opportunity to talk about them, I shouldn't keep quiet or conceal them, otherwise I might be as ungrateful as that bad servant in the New Testament.[62]

DON PEDRO: You're doing just as you should. Ingratitude is a very wicked offence. But let's get back to what we were talking about. I think it's an unusually pleasant subject. Tell me, are Tortosa's arms still the ones with the ship in full sail?

LIVIO: No. As those who settled here more recently didn't know about that ancient fact, they asked the count for a coat of arms and were given *Gules a Tower with four Merlons Argent therein two Windows above a Gateway Sable.*

DON PEDRO: It's a pity they didn't know a fact that was as important as that. If I were a Tortosan, I'd keep that first coat of arms in the city offices, together with the present one. The kingdom of Aragon keeps all the ones their kings had, together with the current one.

LIVIO: I agree it would be a very good idea to do that, and it's actually necessary if the citizens don't deliberately wish to lose the object of

---

[62] The reference is to the parable of the talents (Matt 24: 14-30; Luke 19, 12-27).

greatest honour and esteem that I know of or that any town in Spain can possess.

DON PEDRO: That's perfectly true. And what you were saying about the sea reaching as far inland as Amposta in ancient times — is that really so? How do you know? Today, as you can see, it's two leagues from the castle of Amposta to the sea.

LIVIO: From what can be seen in the whole of that area, and from the drift of the tide that we see every day, and also from what's been written about the point where the royal fleets used to assemble before undertaking voyages, it would look very much as if that's the case — that the sea came as far inland as I've said. What's more, we can see that the shore that the sea reached up to is lined with ancient towers, starting with the tower of La Ràpita and going up to the tower or castle of Camarles. Today, if you just dig a little, you can find remains on all those fringes that it left behind. That's especially true of La Granadella, a fortified tower located on the very edge, about half a league from the sea, where, in the past few years, they've found sea shells and sea crabs. And at Campredó, another fortified tower which, as I said earlier, is way above Amposta and a league from Tortosa, they've found very similar remains. There isn't a single place on that fringe where they haven't found evidence for this. We also know that the French King Peter's fleet, when it got back from Africa and Sicily, and Prince Alfonso's fleet that conquered the island of Sardinia for his father King James — which Pope Boniface had given him, and the conquest of which was carried out at the earnest request and petition of Count Hugh, judge of Arborea and viscount of Barcelona[63] — and what Peter III did in order to retake Sardinia (which, thanks to the treachery of that same judge of Arborea, had rebelled), and what Martín, duke of Montblanc did (the one who later became king) in order to go and reign in Sicily together with his son, Prince Martin, and Queen Mary of Sicily, his daughter-in-law, the prince's wife, when all three of them reigned there: all their fleets and armadas gathered at Port Fangós, which today is no longer a port, but a great lake, now known as Lo Pantà. And there are plenty more lakes, all of which were left behind when the sea retreated. Besides, it's proved quite clearly by the fact that, over the past sixty

---

[63] In fact, Hugh was not viscount of Barcelona. This error is thought to have arisen from the fact that a later judge of Arborea was viscount of Narbone.

years, the cape of L'Aluet has stretched out a good league towards the tower of La Ràpita, the same way that, in time to come, the sea will take the same course and close the port of Els Alfacs, which today is very big. That's why we consider, and it's obvious, that when Tubal reached the Ebro, the sea covered Amposta and Campredó, which are almost the same place.

DON PEDRO: What can have made them become so far removed from the sea?

LIVIO: The river flows so fast that, with all the storms and spate floods, it moves the sea further away, day by day, and it won't stop doing that for as long as the world endures.

DON PEDRO: I can well believe it, and that makes me even more convinced by what you've said about Tortosa being the first settlement to be established in Spain, even if Florián de Ocampo says the opposite.

LIVIO: If you think about it carefully, what Florián says about it doesn't exactly contradict what I've been saying, even though his intention is to honour his own nation, because amongst the things that those Castilians do in comparison with other peoples is this: in order to attribute as much honour as possible to themselves, they either conceal or they disguise the truth, or else they just tell plain lies. Here's what Florián says, in Book IV, chapter III: that, when Tubal had assigned the companies that arrived with him in Andalusia, some of them went back again to visit the first provinces in Spain that they'd passed through. And he goes on to say that that's how they got to the province that would later be called Catalonia, which shows that it's here that Tubal arrived before any other part of Spain. And, if it was, it would be incredible if he hadn't founded a settlement on such a pleasant and fertile piece of land, on such an important and delightful bank as here on the Ebro. And it's perfectly true that Florián doesn't say that Tubal didn't establish settlements earlier in other parts of Spain than in Andalusia and Portugal. What he says is that Andalusia was the first province in which he deliberately made settlements.

DON PEDRO: That's fine. Tortosa finally was established by Tubal! The city's certainly got an ancient founder — so ancient, in fact, that his back teeth can't be aching much anymore! Was the city a real stronghold, and was it very large in earlier times?

LIVIO: If you reckon what it was like when it was no bigger than is indicated by the old walls, which are still visible inside the city, it certainly was a sturdy stronghold, and that's what those who wrote about it in those times thought, because it was protected all the way round — on one side, by the castle, which in those days was extremely strong, as it still is today, and on the other side by this great river, which is like an impregnable moat, but I don't regard it as being so well protected now, because of the way it's spread out towards the *padrastres*.[64]

Don Pedro: What do you mean by spread out? Is it any bigger now than it used to be?

Livio: The walls are longer than they once were, because the people who settled here after the last conquest realised that the city was so close to the mountain of El Sitjar, just in front of us here, the most dangerous *padrastre* anywhere around and the most difficult to defend, that they decided to extend the walls to include it, so now it's inside the city bounds — the same way that, as they say, Barcelona wanted to include Montjuïc inside its city walls — and that's why today Tortosa's walls are longer than they used to be. I've had them measured, and it turns out that they're over five thousand yards long. None the less, I don't think there are more inhabitants now than there were when they extended the city and settled the land beyond the old walls. Although it isn't very clear whether it was very big or not, there are reliable enough documents that suggest it was a large town with a very illustrious reputation. First of all there's what Pliny writes. He calls Tortosa "*celeberrima*", an epithet that doesn't sound as though it would describe a small place. And, in the chronicle of the conquest of Almeria and Tortosa that the Genoese wrote in their own language, when they come to talk about how Tortosa was divided up, these are the precise words that they used in Genoese: "*Furone fate le parti, un tercio a genovesi et doi terci al conte, e ritornò l'armada en Genova col triompho de doi popolose e magne città.*" We also read that King Louis of France, Charlemagne's son, sailed up the Ebro with a large fleet and besieged Tortosa but couldn't take it. From which it follows that Tortosa was either big or strong, or both. Mossèn Francès Tarafa, a canon of Barcelona, in the book that he's written recently entitled *De origine ac rebus gestis regum Hispaniae*, when he comes to describe the source and the course of the Ebro, says: "Joined by the Cinca and the Segre, the Ebro flows past the very rich city of Tortosa."[65] But what goes to show more than anything else that Tortosa was big is the act of donation of

---

[64] A little later on, Livio explains the meaning of this word as the mountains to the east of Tortosa.

[65] In the original, the quotation is in Latin.

the cathedral made by the Catholic King Ildefonso of Aragon in 1178 that's kept in the cathedral archive and which begins like this:

Blessed be God, merciful Father, great and worthy of praise, who, after much devastation, after many tribulations of war, visited His places at the opportune moment... You all know that the city of Tortosa, a royal and episcopal seat from ancient times, passed, for our sins, from the law and authority of the Christians to the power of the Mohammedans. This city, the glory of Spain, which, thanks to its situation, tall mountains, great number of inhabitants, crossed by the river Ebro, is considered to be almost impregnable, adored the living God, our Lord Jesus Christ. But, in the end, the grace of the Holy Spirit infused the breast of the illustrious and ever victorious Ramon Berenguer, count of Barcelona, prince of Aragon, marquis of Provence, and the divine will inspired in him the conquest of the impregnable city of Tortosa. Finally, when he had gathered together many thousands of soldiers, both cavalry and footmen, he besieged the city, assaulted it and won. Without delay, with the favour of divine clemency, Tortosa was taken: the key of the Christians, glory of the peoples, jewel of the entire earth. There the ancient cathedral was restored and dedicated by the archbishop of Tarragona in honour of the Virgin Mary, our Holy Lady Mother of God, in the year 1178 of the incarnation of the Lord, eleventh Indiction, 4 of the Calends of December.[66]

DON PEDRO: The records you've quoted to us, Livio, are quite admirable. They'd be enough for the most prominent city in Spain to be proud of. But, before I forget, I'd just like to ask you what you mean by the word *padrastres?*

LIVIO: It's those mountains that are close to the eastern end of the city that we call Les Bastides, and the hill that's in front of the Vilanova Turret, that rise up above the city. That's why, during the war that the whole of Catalonia waged against King John not many years ago, the people of Tortosa were forced to build a castle-like fortress on Les Bastides in order to defend it from that mountain, and they quartered three hundred men there to prevent the enemy occupying it, which was a really sensible precaution.

FABIO: But the city was taken, all the same.

---

[66] In the original, the text is cited in Latin.

LIVIO: That's true, but, if it hadn't been for that, it would have been taken right away, with great ferocity, and the whole population would have been slaughtered. In fact, it fell after a truce was negotiated, so it was given up by treaty, without anyone getting hurt. That was made possible by rebutting the first onslaught; otherwise, it would have been a disaster.

DON PEDRO: So why don't you keep those defences in good order in case they're needed again, as you've demonstrated how important they were for the protection of the city?

LIVIO: As we're no longer on the frontier, we don't reckon we need to fear a surprise attack. If an enemy comes along, provided it isn't all of a sudden, those defences can quickly be put back in order.

FABIO: Please God we may never need to fear that. For now, there's no need to worry, as we're well prepared. When the kingdom of Valencia was held by the Moors, the people of Tortosa were right on the frontier and in a worrying situation. Although there's never any lack of Moorish or Turkish raids along the coast, they're never successful, and the fact is we also play nasty tricks on them, like in 1523 when three ships of theirs were captured, together with all the rigging and all the Turks and the Christian captives on board; and in 1547 a galliot was taken, with seventy-two Turks on board, and a hundred and fifty captives were freed; and in 1553 a large galliot was rammed at the cape of Els Alfacs, with our men right in the face of the artillery on open flat land, and some Turks were killed and twenty-one Christian prisoners were captured when they'd been thrown out on land to dry some sails, and the sails were captured, as were two guard dogs that the captain had with him, and the ship had to raise anchor in a great hurry and with its bows smashed in. And on innumerable occasions we've taken prisoner four, six or ten Turks, using wily ruses to ambush them. Yes, don't you imagine that we just let them get off scot free![67]

DON PEDRO: From what you say, you must all be used to handling arms.

FABIO: You can be quite sure of that!

DON PEDRO: Going back to what we were saying about those defences at Les Bastides that were built during the war against King John, I'd like to know how it happened and what disaster befell to make

---

[67] Despuig was involved directly in the defence of the district in his capacity as captain of one of the city's military companies.

people as loyal as the Catalans, and so inclined and accustomed to the service of their princes at all times, fall, as fall they did, into such a misfortune as to make war on their lord, King John. Everyone who learns about it and who has heard of the Catalan nation is truly horrified.

LIVIO: That whole business is such an enormous labyrinth that I don't know whether even Ariadne would be capable of helping a man get out of it, if once he entered.[68] That's why it will be best if we don't discuss it just now.

DON PEDRO: No, I insist. You must tell me. I beg you as earnestly as I can to do me this favour, because I'm dying to know about it, and I've been looking for someone for days who'll tell me, and I've never managed to find anyone. As I know full well that you can do so at least as well as anyone else, stop looking for excuses to avoid taking on the task, especially as amongst the three of us we can talk about whatever we like. Besides, the people whom it might affect are no longer alive, and there's more leeway and freedom to talk about it with the living, as long as we tell the truth. All these arguments ought to move and convince you to accede to my request.

FABIO: Look, if it can be told without harming us, I too beg you to do so. And, if not, let's just drop the subject, as it's sensible not to want to hear things that will make one unhappy, if there's no way they can be changed.

LIVIO: I was only hesitating because I didn't want to risk getting involved in the embarrassment or the hazards that you fear. Regarding the first thing *you* mentioned, Don Pedro, I can assure you that I shan't stray from the truth, as there's no reason why anyone who is reasonable and dispassionate should fear it, and I haven't got much time for those who aren't. And, as for what *you* say, Fabio, about it being something that can be discussed without harm to our nation, I say it certainly can be talked about without doing any harm at all. There's no need to doubt that for a moment. But I shan't do so, because it's a big subject, and we'd need to be relaxed and in a quiet, peaceful place. Now it's late, and we're here on the bridge in the middle of a crowd of people, and we've chatted more than enough already. It would be a better idea if we went and had a meal and then, tomorrow morning, when we get up and get dressed, if you still want to talk

---

[68] The reference is to the Greek myth of Ariadne helping Theseus to find his way out of the Minotaur's labyrinth.

about it, we can do so at our leisure until it's time to go to mass, as Fabio won't want to miss that.

FABIO: Definitely not! And I want to hear what you have to say more than anyone.

DON PEDRO: Livio, you're quite right. What a good idea it is to go and have something to eat and put an end to our conversation for now. Let's go straight to your house.

The Fifth Dialogue

THE FIFTH DIALOGUE, WHICH TREATS OF THE WAR THAT THE PRINCIPALITY OF CATALONIA WAGED AGAINST KING JOHN II BECAUSE OF THE CAPTURE AND DEATH OF PRINCE CHARLES, AND IN WHICH THE DEFENCE IS ARGUED FOR THE CATALAN NATION AND THE REASONS ARE GIVEN WHY WAR WAS DECLARED. THE SPEAKERS ARE THE SAME.

Speakers:
FABIO, a gentleman; DON PEDRO, a Valencian;
LIVIO, a knight.

FABIO: I see it's still very quiet in this room. Don't you intend getting up today? Hey! Good day to both of you!

DON PEDRO: Who goes there? Oh! Fabio! I wish you a very good day! You've caught us unawares!

FABIO: Well, it's the early bird that catches the worm!

LIVIO: I too wish you a good day, though I'd prefer not to. Shush! I'll bet Fabio was afraid we'd start up a conversation without him!

FABIO: To tell you the truth, I couldn't stop thinking about it, because last night Don Pedro seemed to be so eager to hear how that war between Catalonia and King John came about that I thought he'd have kept on nagging you about it until he'd heard the whole story.

LIVIO: Didn't I tell you how anxious Fabio is about everything? There's no-one like him!

DON PEDRO: Well, it's alright now. And, as we're here alone, let's lose no more time. Come on, Livio! Start telling us the story before anything else gets in the way. The best way to avoid interruptions is just to get on with the job. But it's going to have to be on one condition — that afterwards we'll go on to talk about what's still left to hear about Tortosa and its environs, and I think there must still be plenty left to tell.

LIVIO: Fabio will have to promise you that, as well as me, as I think he knows at least as much as I do about what's left to be told. It's to do with things that can be seen, and he must be more familiar with those, because he's resided here more regularly than I have.

FABIO: Let's not waste time on that. We'll explain everything we know, just as long as we don't forget anything!

LIVIO: Look, as you're both commanding me to go into that battle, I just want to warn you that I shan't talk about the whole course of the war, because that would be an infinitely long affair, and very tedious, and also because it's already been written about by Lucio Marineo and by Don Jeroni Sans, abbot of Benifassà, and others, so it would be a waste of time. I'll only deal with its causes and with why the Catalans stood out so conspicuously in that action, as I take it that that's what you're asking about, Don Pedro. So let's be quite clear — tell me if that's really what you want.

DON PEDRO: That's exactly it, because I've already read about what happened in the war, and I've seen that those who write about it don't speak well of the Catalans. In fact, they keep on speaking very badly of them, treating them as disloyal, as rebels, as traitors, and using a thousand other insults, and that's insufferable for such an honourable nation. Which is why I'm amazed that the people of Catalonia can put up with books like those and don't try to get them all burnt. And that's why I want to hear what justification can be put forward for them, seeing the affection and the devotion that you know I feel towards this nation. That's what I'm asking for.

LIVIO: Very well, then. If that's how it is, I hope in God that this time you'll get satisfaction and start thinking differently from what you've been persuaded to believe up to now. And I shan't tell lies or go in for malice, as Lucio Marineo and others have done who've written about that war — writers who, just to praise and flatter the king, haven't thought twice about defaming this nation which, as you've just said, Don Pedro, is as loyal and courageous as any in Spain, and more unstinting and generous in its princes' service than any in the whole of Europe. And I trust that neither of you will hesitate to contradict me at any point, as that will help me to explain myself better, and will help you to understand and get to know the truth.

DON PEDRO: So be it!

LIVIO: Well, then, please listen. To help you to understand better, I'll start just a little way upstream. King John — about whom we're going to speak, as you know — was the son of Ferdinand I, King Martin's heir and successor in the kingdom of Aragon.[69] He was a courteous prince: merciful, wise, pious and strong. He married twice — first, Queen Blanca, the daughter and heiress of Charles III, the Noble, king of Navarre. They had a son, who was given the title of prince of Viana and who, in his day, was one of the most courtly and excellent princes in the whole world: beloved, cherished, doted on and idolised by all the princes of France, Italy and Spain, as well as by the Pope, who held him most dear. He was better endowed than any other prince of his time with nobility, moderation, greatness of spirit, knowledge, courage and virtue. He possessed (and it showed) greatness to the highest degree, and — as his uncle, the wise and magnanimous King Alfonso often said — he knew more than any other king on earth. In terms of generosity and liberality, he was so far ahead of any other king that, even without a kingdom, he seemed to be more of a king than any of the others. He was such an elegant poet, such a splendid host of foreign guests, and such an exquisite devisor of courtly celebrations and festivities, that everyone wanted to follow and serve him. The knowledge of noble pursuits and royal and courtly accomplishments shone so brightly in his palace that all men of honour and valour were drawn to it, as to a school of genteel and perfect breeding. Besides that, he was such a good Christian and so devout that he was regarded as a saint. Ferdinand's second wife was Queen Joan, the daughter of Don Federic Enríquez, Admiral of Castile, and by her he had Prince Ferdinand of Aragon, whom we call king of Sicily and who later became king of Aragon, known as the Catholic monarch, the most outstanding and the most fortunate king that the kingdom of Aragon has ever had.

Well, when King John was away from Navarre on the Naples campaign — which he undertook together with his brother King Alfonso of Aragon, whom he wished to support, when that kingdom was conquered, as well as afterwards, when he governed those kingdoms for Alfonso — he entrusted the government of the kingdom of Navarre to his second wife, Queen Joan. Prince Charles took offence at the way his father had entrusted to his stepmother the kingdom that he would inherit via his mother, and he felt as if he'd been disinherited, as if he were a rogue. And, as he was in the right, as I've explained,

69 He was John II, 'the Great' (1398-1479).

even though in his first youth he pretended to ignore the offence, when he came of age he could stand the affront no longer and sent to entreat his father, King John, to insult him no more by withholding from him the government of the kingdom of Navarre which should have been his, as heir to his mother, Queen Blanca of Navarre, claiming that by doing so he seemed to be demonstrating to the world that he, his son, was incompetent or suffered from some kind of incapacity, and that if, up to that moment, his youth could have been regarded as a reason for his ill-treatment, now that he was of age there was no excuse for the offence. So he begged his father to be gracious and pleased to command that he be given the government of that kingdom, because it befitted his honour, reputation and authority, assuring his Majesty that he was obliged to make that request, not by lust for power, but by those other considerations. These and other no less weighty points were included in the embassy he sent, though I'll leave them out in order not to be too long-winded.

DON PEDRO: As far as I can see, the prince was right.

LIVIO: Absolutely! But the king took no notice. Instead, after that he was unpleasant towards the prince, his son, on every possible occasion. The noble spirit of the virtuous prince was unable to stand that, and so — supported by the Portuguese, by one of the two main factions in Navarre and by King Henry of Castile — he determined to remove his stepmother from the government of the kingdom. When King John, who at the time was over here, heard of that, he speedily invaded Navarre with as large a force as he could muster. After a few skirmishes between father and son, the prince was finally captured in battle and taken to the castle of Montroig, in Aragon, and then to the castle of Morella, in Valencia, where, thanks to the intervention of several prelates and noblemen, he was set free and returned to the king's grace, and they signed an agreement regarding the government of Navarre. However, when the prince later insisted that the agreement hadn't been honoured and the queen took up the government of the kingdom again, he decided to reopen the earlier quarrel, though he fared no better than before, except that, as this time he wasn't captured, he went to Naples, where his uncle King Alfonso reigned — the one who, as I said before, was also king of Aragon and who loved him dearly. When, however, King Alfonso died just a few days later, the prince resolved to go to Sicily, whilst his father, King John, succeeded Alfonso in all the kingdoms of the Crown of Aragon, except for Naples, where Ferdinand, Alfonso's natural son, became king. And, since King John was still enraged by the prince, the latter thought it best to stay in Sicily, where the Sicilians treated him with great courtesy and put on many festivities in his honour.

DON PEDRO: You've left me quite bewildered, Livio, by what you've been saying. I really don't understand how that could come about. On the one hand, you tell us that King John was a wise, forgiving and pious monarch, and on the other you demonstrate so many perfect accomplishments and qualities on the part of Prince Charles that it would seem to be impossible to speak better of any man — although (to tell you the truth) I'm afraid you may have laid the praise on a bit too thick — and then you tell us that King John persecuted his splendid son with such fury and so unjustly and unreasonably. For my part, as I say, I just don't understand it. If the king really was so wise, he should never have started. And if he was so forgiving and pious, he shouldn't have carried on.

LIVIO: I haven't invented what I've been saying about the prince. It's all in the *Chronicle of Aragon*, written by Friar Gualberte Fabricio de Vagad, of the Order of St. Bernard, in his life of John II. He was a contemporary of Prince Charles, and he worked hard and conscientiously to write the chronicle, at the request and at the expense of the Diputats of the kingdom of Aragon. As for what they say about the king, I agree with you, but the facts are just as I've told them.

FABIO: Perhaps the prince — even if he was just as Livio has described him — was too young to rule. We know full well what a disaster it is when kingdoms fall into the hands of men who are too young.

LIVIO: What do you mean by too young? No, in fact he was of a perfectly proper age, over thirty-three years old, and he had as elegant a judgement as any man of his time.

DON PEDRO: Goodness! From now on, I'll do my best to get this right. If the prince was that old, why on earth did the king get so angry with him, and why did his anger last so long?

FABIO: Yes, why indeed?

DON PEDRO: Because of the opinions and the disagreements of Queen Joan. After all, she was a stepmother.

LIVIO: You've hit the nail on the head. That's exactly the reason. There's no other.

FABIO: What made the queen behave so badly?

LIVIO: First of all, as I've said, she was a stepmother. Secondly, she had a son of her own by the king, namely Prince Ferdinand, and she was determined that he should reign after her husband, and that wasn't possible as long as Prince Charles was alive, as he was the first born. And it was out of that ambition and passion of hers that her son should become king that she planned against innocent Prince Charles all the malice she was capable of, and carried on like that up to the point that I'm just going to tell you about.

DON PEDRO: Carry on! We're engrossed by what you're telling us.

LIVIO: The principality of Catalonia, which is where the main power and force of the Crown lay, was most distressed by what it saw going on between its king and the prince, as one of them was already their monarch and the other was to be so in good time. It therefore decided to try to reconcile them and sent a solemn embassy to the king, begging him in effect to forgive the prince and to take him back into his affection and favour. The king was pleased to oblige the Catalans, forgave the prince for what had happened and solemnly promised them that, from that moment on, he would treat his son the prince with fatherly love and protect and defend his person and his honour and authority like his own. When he'd done that with all the appropriate formality, the principality sent seven galleys at its own expense to Sicily, where the prince was still living, to inform him about what had been agreed and to ask him to come over here to Catalonia. Although he was always suspicious of his stepmother, the prince was given such solid assurance by the Catalan ambassadors, speaking in the name of the entire principality, that he agreed to come over, and sailed to Barcelona with those seven galleys.

DON PEDRO: What you're saying, Livio, is news to me. As I said, I've read all about that war in Lucio Marineo, but he doesn't say a thing about what you're telling us — that the Catalans dared get involved in those disputes, or that the king gave them his word about anything, or that they brought the prince back to Catalonia.

LIVIO: It's perfectly true that he says nothing about it, and that's where his malice and his meanness and his wickedness come out most clearly. In order to pile as much blame as possible on the Catalans and to remove it from the king, he didn't say a word about what had been discussed or what had gone on before. In particular, he kept quiet about the Catalans sending over the seven galleys to bring the prince back at their own expense, so that no-one in the future should think that on that account the Catalans had had any cause for complaint, so eager was he to lay the blame on the Catalans. And he even had the shameless effrontery to say that it was the prince who sent an embassy from Sicily to ask pardon of the king and that, as soon as he obtained it, he returned to Catalonia accompanied by a whole lot of Sicilians, without wishing to record that, as I've said, it was Catalans who went to fetch him or that it was Catalans who accompanied him, the opposite of what he says being so well known that there's no-one who's unaware of it. Nor, in all his work, does he say a word about the regal qualities or the admirable character of the prince, and all just so that there shouldn't be the slightest letting up in the guilt that he piles on the Catalans. Now, with all these facts that he deliberately leaves out, you can appreciate the malice and the twisted intentions that inspired that Sicilian writer Marineo. How could anyone believe that the prince would have trusted the king so easily, just like that, as he says, seeing that he'd had to cope with all the evil traps and plots that the queen had set for him? The fact is that, in spite of all the assurances he got from the Catalans, who at that time enjoyed the reputation throughout Europe of being like new Romans, he didn't trust them, as I say, and he wouldn't have trusted them without the powerful insistence of their ambassadors and the confidence he had in the support and the valour of the Catalans. And that was the real point, the major spur, that later moved the Catalans to do what they did, considering that it was because of the confidence he had placed in them that the prince had come over and had suffered.

DON PEDRO: He had every reason to inform himself well. I, for one, wouldn't have had much confidence, and I can say that the Catalans got caught up in an awful labyrinth. I don't see why they didn't think more carefully about what they were doing, seeing how canny and unhurried and cautious they usually are.

LIVIO: It was because they didn't think about it enough that so many calamities and misfortunes overcame them afterwards, and they lost nearly half of Catalonia. As they were already deep in the mud, they decided to trample through it with great valour and energy.

FABIO: Who wouldn't have trusted a king, especially when it came to promises made for his son's benefit?

DON PEDRO: But a son who'd seen and experienced the tricks and traps set by his stepmother.

LIVIO: In the end, as I said, the prince landed here in Catalonia and went to kiss his father's hands and humbled himself with great courtesy before the queen, his stepmother. There were great festivities and rejoicing to mark his arrival, and everything changed so much that it seemed as if the past would be consigned to oblivion. However, the queen, who was desperate to make her son rule, was infuriated by what she saw, even though she pretended not to be, and arranged for a message to reach the king to the effect that the prince was planning to have him murdered.

DON PEDRO: Jesus! Is it possible that such infamy could be imputed to as good and saintly a person as you've said the prince was? And did the king actually come to believe it?

LIVIO: The king did believe it, and he immediately ordered the arrest of the prince, who at the time was in Lleida, where the king was holding his Parliament with the Catalans, and had him taken to the Aljafería, in Saragossa, where he was held under close arrest.

DON PEDRO: What must Catalonia have been and felt like at that instant, seeing itself so affronted, with the pledge made to its beloved prince shattered, and him detained and so harshly treated, at a moment when Catalonia was so well populated that it was bursting open like a pomegranate?

LIVIO: You can imagine how the Parliament reacted that had been called together in Lleida. It sent three ambassadors to beg the king to set the prince free, and elected twenty-seven men from the three estates with powers to negotiate, deliberate, supplicate and do and spend whatever they thought necessary in order to get the prince freed, arranging and providing for those representatives to go to Barcelona to meet at the palace of the Diputació, where, as representatives of the whole of Catalonia, they were to do whatever was required. When they met there, they decided to send more ambassadors and chose twelve men who, together with three from the Parliament at Lleida, made a total of fifteen, all of whom begged the king to free the prince and complained about the way he'd broken his word. When he told them that the answer was no, the Diputats put on more pressure and sent, in addition to the twenty-seven men they'd sent before, forty-five additional ambassadors, making a total of sixty. But the king still wouldn't budge. Instead, fearing that the ambassadors meant to arrest him, he left Lleida on foot by night, just before dinner, leaving the tables laid, and went to Fraga and then on to Saragossa.

DON PEDRO: What a foolish thing to do! The ambassadors and the Parliament gathered there must have been dumbfounded.

LIVIO: Never had anything more terrible or despicable been seen! The people walked about the streets in shock, confusion and bewilderment, staring at each other, incapable of offering advice or suggesting a remedy.

DON PEDRO: So what happened in the end?

LIVIO: Seeing how King John closed his ears and absolutely refused to listen to such just requests, and how there was nothing to be gained by words, the principality of Catalonia decided to take action and rapidly put together a powerful army, with the count of Mòdica in command, and ordered it to march at once to the place where the prince was being held and free him by force of arms. When the king heard that, fearing worse trouble, he ordered the prince to be set free without delay, and that's what happened. However, the Catalans weren't satisfied with that and wanted the prince to be given full government and command over Catalonia, with the king being left as sovereign in name only, and the people swearing loyalty only to the prince. In order to make sure of that, a formal treaty was signed by the king and the principality, and, when the matter had been resolved and concluded in the Catalans' favour, the prince came over to Catalonia, and then to Barcelona, in triumph and to the great joy of all the people and, from then on, ruled as sovereign lord without any kind of opposition.

DON PEDRO: The Catalans really ended the matter splendidly. They were truly praiseworthy. There's no getting away from it — they've always been men of integrity and probity, and zealous in defence of their honour. So how did the clock go wrong again?

LIVIO: Let me tell you. When all of that had happened and things had gone as you've heard, the queen — an intrepid and passionate monarch who was indignant about what was happening and was determined to carry out her evil plan to make her son Fernando king after her husband, which was impossible so long as Charles was alive — decided that, one way or another, she would have Prince Charles killed, and she actually had him given poison, from which he died less than three days later.

DON PEDRO: What frightful cruelty! What a dastardly deed! What pestilent ambition! It's that rabid greed for power that deranges and blinds all mortals! Not even a Nero, or a Sulla, or a Herod, or a

Pontius Pilate, or those kings of Castile, Sancho IV and Peter the Cruel, would have wrought such cruelty or such execrable evil! I know full well that Queen Eleanor (the second wife of King Alfonso, the one who conquered Sardinia), in order to enable her son Ferdinand (who was marquis of this city of Tortosa) to rule over a large part of the kingdom of Valencia, instead of Peter (the king's first son by his first wife), took the risk of losing the whole of the Crown of Aragon, but at least she didn't attempt anything as evil or diabolical as that.

FABIO: I expect, Livio, it's those who supported Prince Charles who make those accusations against Queen Joan, but it couldn't be that easy to get people to believe them. You know the saying: "People always exaggerate, whether it's for or against."

LIVIO: I wasn't there at the time, so I can't claim to be an eyewitness. All I can tell you is what I've heard, and that's the opinion that's generally held to be correct. I remember the first lines of a song that was sung everywhere, on account of all that, for many years, the lines that go: "May God be pleased to cleanse the washing done in myrtle water." And they sang that because it was believed that it was in myrtle water that he'd been given the poison. Some said it had been administered some other way, but what everyone agreed about was that it had been done very treacherously. What you can find in writings and in the judicial documents is that, a few days after it left his body, the Prince's soul wandered through Barcelona for several nights screaming out aloud and making it known that the queen, his stepmother, had had him poisoned, moaning loudly as if it was demanding that justice be done.

DON PEDRO: That would have been a ghost of some kind, or some sort of trick.

LIVIO: I don't know about that, but I do know this — all of Catalonia believed it and took it to be true, which is why they decided to rise up against the king and queen, declaring them, by way of a solemn proclamation made first in Barcelona and then throughout Catalonia, enemies of the people.

DON PEDRO: That was really something terrible! And what reasons did they give?

LIVIO: I don't know what reasons they gave in the proclamation, but these are the reasons why they declared war. First, because the king had broken his word when he'd pledged to protect and safeguard the person and the honour of the prince like his own when the principality of Catalonia sent the seven galleys to bring him over, and the king, breaking his promise, had then had him arrested in Lleida, as I told you. Secondly, because he'd contravened the constitution, having the prince arrested in the principality and then removed, along with Don Juan de Beamunt, Prior of Navarre, and Gomes de Frías, who were detained with him. Thirdly, because he'd broken the agreement he'd made and sworn with the Catalans over those matters, in particular pledging that he wouldn't enter Catalonia unless he was asked to by the principality, and then doing so none the less, for which reason he'd immediately been publicly declared a private subject and an enemy of the people. Fourth, and last, above all, because he'd ordered the prince, their lord, to be murdered.

DON PEDRO: Those certainly are powerful arguments, but don't the first ones refer to previous matters over which the parties had arrived at an accord, when the prince was handed over to the Catalans and was given absolute power and command over the whole of Catalonia? If so, why did they base their arguments on things that no longer applied?

LIVIO: It's quite true, as you say, that they were concerned with previous matters, but you know too that, even when evil deeds are pardoned and forgiven, if others are perpetrated later, those that were forgiven are added to the new ones and aggravate the new crime. That's why they wished, and were able, to combine the last iniquitous crime with the ones he'd committed earlier against the Catalans. Don't you think, then, that those were perfectly just reasons for them to take up arms?

DON PEDRO: I've heard some Valencian, and even some Catalan, knights claim that what was done to free the prince was fine, but that what was done after his death wasn't necessary.

LIVIO: What you're saying, Don Pedro, obliges me to rise in my saddle and sharpen my quill if I'm to answer you and correct the opinion of the people who say that, and I know there are those who do. The first thing I'd say is this: that those who say that either believe that the Catalans were wrong to get involved in the disagreements between the king and the prince or in the promise made to them by the king, or else they don't. If that's what they say, then they can't conceivably be right, because it's obvious that, if they had the right to protest about the prince's arrest despite the assurances they'd received, they were even more right to protest about his death, because the damage and the offence were far greater. And, if they don't think the Catalans overstepped the mark or that they were given assurances regarding the prince, I say that in neither case were the Catalans right to get involved in anything to do with this. If not, just tell me: for what reason should the principality get involved in anything to do with the king's actions towards his son? Any such proceedings would be completely gratuitous. It may, and it should, plead with him in his son's favour, but if the king wishes to do nothing, there's no need or obligation whatever for the kingdom to try to oblige him, especially given the fact that Catalonia isn't the entire Crown of Aragon, or even the head of it, so there's no reason why it should load on its own back such a heavy, fearful and terrible burden. So, if the Catalans didn't overstep the mark and no kind of pledge had been given them, they were just as wrong in what they did when the prince was arrested as when he was killed. However, if they did go too far in that, and if they'd been given assurances, I say they were free, and even obliged, to do what they did when he was detained and, for just the same reason, what they did when he was murdered. And the same praise and honour up to the horns of the moon that were accorded to the Catalans by everyone because of what they did when he was arrested would have been well deserved, or even more so, because of what they did when he was killed. And, if not, they deserved none on either account.

Thus, Don Pedro, the argument of those knights you referred to lacks any kind of reason or force, though it's true and perfectly well known that the Catalans did get involved in those quarrels and that, through their intervention, the king and the prince were brought together and reconciled. And it's for precisely that reason that they were the first to discover just how the prince had been murdered — as I said, poisoned — and were then able to take action in respect of that, and they did well to do so. And I'd go further. Thinking about the prudence, the experience and the maturity of the Catalan nation, which they display in everything they do, and, in addition, their innate loyalty towards their kings and lords, as such memorable acts prove and proclaim, a loyalty that kings have openly acknowledged at all times, any person of good judgement is bound to accept that they must have had perfectly good reasons to break with that king, and there isn't conceivably one single riposte or rebuttal or contradiction to be made against that.

DON PEDRO: All that's fine, but, according to what you've been saying, the king wasn't to blame for the murder, if the queen had arranged it, assuming you really believe that.

LIVIO: I certainly do believe it. If he died poisoned, it was mainly thanks to the schemes plotted by his stepmother, the queen, but with the king's acquiescence, for the reasons I've given you, and that's what everyone said. What's more, as regards his stepmother, I've heard from a most reverent and important lady, whose name I don't wish to divulge, that some pious and, by all accounts, saintly women who founded the Convent of Jerusalem in Barcelona, told the first nuns of that convent — and from them it was passed on to those who live there today — that they'd had a revelation that said that Queen Joan wasn't on the road to Salvation, that (that being so) it looked as if that was the punishment for that crime, and she herself had shown that that was what would happen by what she'd said shortly before she died, conscience-stricken.

DON PEDRO: And what did she say, for heavens' sake?

LIVIO: I'll tell you. Taking her son, Prince Ferdinand, by the hand, she said to him: "Ah, my son, you're staying here, as you know, to reign. But, wretched me, I must go, perhaps to suffer in torment."

FABIO: That's really bizarre. Can that really have happened?

LIVIO: I say that that's what I was told, and people believe it to be true.

FABIO: Why on earth would those women have wanted to get tangled up in a thing like that?

LIVIO: Because it was that queen who set up the convent at their suggestion, and it was she who ordered the church to be built that's still there — actually, it looks too poor to be the work of a queen — and that's why they were so keen to find out about what had happened and about the queen's death. As for what you say about not believing that the king was to blame for such a wicked crime, I'd like to believe that, too, because it's hard to imagine that a monarch who was as exceptional as King John was could have had a hand in such an ugly business, but he certainly did to the extent that he showed scarcely any grief over the death, and didn't display the sorrow that he should have done, nor did he want to deny the Catalans' guilt for what he and the queen were accused of by the people, nor would he go along with the claims they made against the queen. On the contrary: by his actions he showed that he was pleased with everything that had happened. So people were bound to believe that the king, too, knew all about the prince's murder, or tacitly went along with it, as I've said. That's why war had to be declared on him, because of the queen, and it lasted ten years, with huge numbers of dead and the destruction of castles and laying waste of towns. In the end, that frenzied war left half of Catalonia depopulated.

DON PEDRO: Whatever you say, I reckon it's a very serious matter to renounce one's loyalty to a king, and even more serious to make open warfare on him. I don't believe anything like that has ever been seen.

LIVIO: But it's an even more serious matter to break a pledge made in such a solemn act, murdering the king himself, since Prince Charles was, in effect, lord of Catalonia, because his father (as I told you) only kept for himself the title of count of Barcelona. So the Catalans were perfectly justified in defending both *their* honour in respect of the oath that had been broken — because "*Frangenti fidem fides frangatur eidem*"[70] — and the honour of their lord and king, which is what the prince was.

As for what you say about nothing like that ever having been seen before, I'm afraid you're seriously mistaken. Either you haven't read terribly much, or else your memory is at fault. In any case, just pointing out obstacles doesn't solve a problem. Let me give you a few examples of similar instances so you can see that there are precedents and that they haven't been treated as wicked or illicit, as you say and seem to believe, so long as reason and justice prevailed. Take Tarquin, king of Rome:[71] the Romans cast off their obedience to his permanent rule and made bloody war on him until they brought about his total ruin and perdition; and they did so, not because he'd affronted all of Rome, as in our case the whole of Catalonia had been affronted, but just one person, and it wasn't even the king who'd offended him, but the king's son, which would be like our case if the queen alone had been involved in the wicked plot. Well, on that score, not only aren't the Romans regarded as traitors or rebels: they're actually held to be honourable and valorous, as indeed they were, and as all their descendents also deserved to be regarded. And in this Spain of ours, King Alfonso X of Castile had his kingdom removed from him, and the Castilians made open warfare against

70 "If someone has broken trust, let your trust in him be broken" (Latin proverb).
71 Tarquinius Superbus (535-496 BC), the legendary seventh and final King of Rome, whose son raped Lucretia.

him, even though he was the wisest, most liberal and magnanimous prince of all those in the world at that time, so much so that nowadays the Castilians refer to him as Alfonso the Wise.[72] Well, as I say, they deprived him of his entire kingdom, so that all he was left with was Seville, and he died disinherited. As for King John, even though the Catalans made him stare into the wolf's mouth and test the sharpness of its teeth, in the end they took him back as their lord and king, and he lived amongst them greatly beloved and was mourned at his death.

FABIO: That isn't a bad example to make those malicious Castilian tongues stop wagging and rattling on at us about that war against King John.

LIVIO: Oh, I could carry on forever if I told you all the things like that that have gone on between the Castilians and their kings! Don't you know what Don Juan de Lanuza, an Aragonese knight who was viceroy of Aragon for many years, said?

FABIO: No, I don't.

LIVIO: Once, when he was in Castile at the table of a lord, talking about certain differences he'd had with a Castilian knight, he said, holding a piece of bread in his hand: "This one piece of bread would sate all the loyal men in Castile and all the traitors in Aragon."

FABIO: That was a remarkably brave thing to say.

LIVIO: You could also say it was true.

DON PEDRO: And I've read that King Peter the Cruel of Castile — when he was near Oriola with a powerful army set against King Peter III of Aragon, who'd gathered an army together there against Castile, and some of the Castilian officers wished to persuade their king to attack — said, with a loaf of bread in his hand that he'd taken from a young boy: "If I had with me the soldiers that the king of Aragon has got, and had them as my vassals, as he's got them, I'd happily fight against all of you and against all Castile." And when, later on, at dinner, they tried again to insist that he attack the following day, he said again: "What excellent advice! All I can say is that, with this piece of bread, I'd satisfy the appetite of all the loyal men in Castile."

LIVIO: That's true. I've read it, too. But, even before that, King Segismund of Hungary, who later became Holy Roman Emperor, had his kingdom taken away by his vassals, who declared war on him

---

[72] Alfonso X, 'the Wise' (1221-1284).

because he'd broken some promises he'd made to them. And, many years before that, at the time of Emperor Henry III, those Hungarians removed King Peter, their natural lord, because he'd ill-treated them and denied them their privileges. And what about Emperor Frederick III, the great-grandfather of our king and lord, Charles V? Didn't his vassals in the dukedom of Austria rise up against him and make pitiless war on him, besieging him in one of his cities with as much fury as if he were a sworn enemy of theirs? And all because he wouldn't set free King Ladislaus of Hungary and Bohemia, whom he was holding prisoner, claiming that he was break-ing the pledge he'd given regarding the freeing of that prince — a case that's very similar to the one we're talking about. I could give you plenty more pertinent examples, but I shan't, because I don't want to upset you and because I reckon I've given you enough already. Think about it. If it's tough for a single honourable person to suffer an affront, it's a lot worse for a whole kingdom, as Marquis Íñigo López de Mendoza puts it so well: "When the good men were conquered, they soon found out how to free their states."

Well, when King John thought all this over and pondered care-fully on it — that peace had been agreed regarding these quarrels and upsets between the twenty-seven men who in Barcelona repre-sented the entire principality of Catalonia, as I said earlier, and the city of Barcelona itself, on the one hand, and King John on the other, and that Queen Joan had died without God allowing her to see her illicit desires prevail — after haggling and wrangling over what grounds would be included in the general concordat regarding the reasons for starting such a furious and violent war (which, as I said, raged for ten whole years), with the king's men wanting it to state that the cause had been the disloyalty and the unwarranted fury of the principality, and the representatives of the principality reject-ing that out of hand and maintaining that it was the king breaking his oath and his word, he tried to justify himself by coming up with the following statement: "Don't say one thing or the other. Just say the war was caused by everyone's sins."

DON PEDRO: That was a brilliant conclusion, worthy of being uttered by a king! So is that how the war came to an end?

LIVIO: That's right. Weighing up how he'd been ill advised and had tried to act brutally and ruthlessly, and seeing that that was why he'd suffered such awful trouble and distress, from then on the king treated the Catalans with such affection and respect and courtesy that he didn't seem to be a king to them at all, but rather a companion and their equal. And that's how they came to have such great affection for him again that, in the war that he fought soon afterwards against the French over the county of Roussillon, everyone in the principality was so impassioned that they came to the aid of the king, who was under siege in Perpignan by the French, and forced the enemy to retire to Narbonne. Think how much more a prince can achieve with his vassals if he treats them with kindness, and not cruelty.

DON PEDRO: That's perfectly true, especially if the vassals are true men, as Spaniards are, and are regarded, in general. And it just goes to prove the pleasing expression used by that brave and magnanimous Emperor Maximilian, who said, as if in jest: "The king of England is a king of devils; the king of France, a king of asses; the king of Spain, a king of men; but I'm a king of kings and not a tyrannical lord." So he regarded Spaniards as men.

FABIO: My goodness! That was a witty thing to say!

LIVIO: He was absolutely right. Believe me, princes need to treat men like men if they want them to act like men. I don't know if I've managed to do what I promised, or if you're satisfied with my explanations. What I do know, though, is that I've been too long-winded about it. I expect I've been boring and annoying you.

DON PEDRO: Not at all! In fact, I'm sorry you've finished. I've really enjoyed listening to you. It's been a great pleasure learning how that whole business came about, to the greater honour of the Catalan nation. As far as I'm concerned, I'm more than satisfied and contented with the defence you've made of the Catalans. It's very different indeed from what I'd thought.

FABIO: I agree entirely. I'd always thought there was no honourable justification for Catalonia's role in that war. Now I see that we can hold our heads high wherever we go, which must be a joy and a pleasure for us all.

LIVIO: That is indeed so. I tell you again: kings must be kings, not tyrants. When we say kings reign, we're referring to the notion *A regendo, a bene regendo*.[73] That's where the word comes from. And reigning ought to imply ruling with a straight ruler. It's all the same word and the same notion. And kings need to keep their promises.

---

73 I.e. "Ruling means ruling well."

Amongst the other wholesome counsels and advice that Aristotle gave Alexander the Great, he told him: "Alexander, *serva pacta!* Keep your word!" And, even though King John was a courteous prince, whether he was influenced by wicked people or for some other reason, he never stopped attributing the beginning of all those misfortunes to his own refusal to allow his son, Prince Charles, to rule Navarre, as it was right and proper that he should. And from that seed there grew all those troubles and all that evil that came about later — "Because, when one thing is discordant, more follow," and, as you know, "Whoever creates the occasion for damage is seen to have done the damage."[74] After that, you can see how serious it was when he broke his pledge, had the prince arrested in Lleida, had him removed from the principality together with those who were detained with him in defiance of the constitutions and privileges, flouting the undertaking he'd given solemnly and under oath not to enter Catalonia and, lastly, murdering him so horribly. These things are truly terrible, frightful and intolerable.

FABIO: They are, indeed, and I've never heard of anything like them.

LIVIO: If only honourable men here would just read, you'd understand these and other matters that are worth remembering and gaining pleasure and profit from. So, from now on, open your eyes, and read as much as you can. It doesn't do any harm to know how things happened in the past. In fact, it helps a lot, and it practically enables those who aren't ignorant to become prophets of the future.

DON PEDRO: What you say is very well spoken, and there's no more to be said about it, except that I'd just like to get one last thing straight to put my mind at rest and to get it clear that, in what you've been explaining, you haven't been moved by passion or bias.

LIVIO: And what exactly do you want to know?

DON PEDRO: I'd just like to hear whether your father, or your grandfather, or anyone else in your family who was alive then, favoured the king or the kingdom.

LIVIO: I can see what you're after. You want to be my father confessor. Well, I'll have you know that it was my grandfather,[75] and he favoured the king. The reason was this: he was the nephew of Don Lluís Despuig, the Master of Montesa, that great favourite of King Alfonso

---

74 In the original, both sayings are in Latin.
75 The reference is to the squire Pere Despuig i Macip.

whom Panormita, in his book *De dictis et factis,* records as having been — as I think, Don Pedro, you'll have heard back in Valencia — such an outstanding and singular person that he left behind him a reputation as a good Master, and that's how he's still known throughout the entire region of Montesa. Well, that Master Don Lluís put my grandfather in charge of the fortress of Peniscola, which at the time belonged to the Order of Montesa, which is why my grandfather found himself there in the midst of that war at the king's service, because the Master, as you'll have guessed, went on serving the king and his household outstandingly and was Queen Joan's and Prince Ferdinand's general in command when the count of Pallars acted in Girona as the general of the whole of Catalonia, demonstrating clearly his personal valour when the enemy broke into the cathedral tower, where the queen had taken shelter, by means of a mine that they'd laid, and made them retreat with great difficulty because of the explosion, leaving behind many dead. And when the castle of Amposta was taken, he was the first man who, by force of arms, gained access to it. So you can believe me: everything I've told you has been said without passion. I haven't been motivated by any intention to defend my own cause. I'm only interested in telling what actually happened.

DON PEDRO: I think that Master was called Don Bernat Despuig.

LIVIO: No, he was called Don Lluís. It's true, there was another one, who was called Don Bernat and who was his nephew, and I actually knew him. He was a notable person. The Catholic King sent him as ambassador to the Pope, and in that capacity he showed that he was a very eminent person, very wise and brave.

DON PEDRO: Now I'm satisfied on every score. I believe you've really been speaking without the prejudice or the bias that I feared, now that I know that your grandfather didn't support the kingdom. In any case, I regard you as someone who's incapable of being moved by his own interests to say anything but the truth. But now I'm even more certain. And, as something else to do with this has just crossed my mind, and I'd also like to know about it, just as much as about all the other things, you must do me the favour of telling me about it, and then we'll finish off this conversation and go and have lunch, because it's twelve o'clock — far too late now to go and hear mass! What I still want to get clear is whether all the Catalans, without exception, went and fought against the king, or did some part or other of the kingdom support him?

Livio: One and all decided to take up arms, and did so — except, that is, for six or seven leading men who, out of respect for him, decided to forget about the country's honour. All the others — that is, the bishops and all the ecclesiastical estate, the counts, viscounts and barons, and the whole of the noble estate, along with all the commons, except for just one or two — took action and persevered in it just as long as they could. And they didn't do so mindlessly, but after thinking about the matter, ruminating and pondering on it very carefully, meeting together on several occasions and weighing everything up with great care. That's exactly why it's right to believe that what the Catalans did was correct, because it was so seriously thought through, and by people who were so clear-headed and so well up in questions to do with matters concerning honour.

Don Pedro: Shush! Let's not spend any more time on this. It's all as clear and well established as it could possibly be. For my part, I couldn't be more satisfied or content.

Fabio: And I just couldn't tell you how happy I am. I want to give you a big hug, Livio, for the good work you've done for our nation, bringing all these facts out into the light. If the Catalans aren't ungrateful, they ought to be indebted to you up to the hilt, and so must this city. As it joined the rest of the principality in waging that war, you've defended the honour of us all.

Livio: Let's leave it at that and go and have a drink. It's high time, and it will do us a lot more good than all this talk.

The Sixth Dialogue

THE SIXTH DIALOGUE, WHICH MANIFESTS THE VARIETY
OF FRUITS AND OTHER EXCELLENT PRODUCE THAT ARE TO BE
FOUND WITHIN THE DISTRICT OF TORTOSA, AND WHICH TREATS
OF THE FIRST INSTITUTIONS THAT CHARLEMAGNE FOUNDED
IN CATALONIA. THE SPEAKERS ARE THE SAME AS APPEAR IN
ALL THE PREVIOUS DIALOGUES.

Speakers:
DON PEDRO, a Valencian; FABIO, a gentleman;
LIVIO, a knight.

DON PEDRO: Livio, I've greatly enjoyed listening to what you've been telling us over lunch about the conquest of Catalonia — who the first people were who came over here after the destruction of Spain at the time of Roderick, the last king of the Goths, and who Otger Golant Catalonico was, namely the leader of the Nine Worthy Barons who were ordained by threes, and who those were who came later and completed the task, which is to say Emperor Charlemagne, king of France, and then Louis, his son, who became king of France after him; and what they say about the name Catalonia, which is that, before the time of Otger Golant, it was called Gotalania and that that name became corrupted and turned into Catalania, and then got corrupted a bit more, and became Catalonia, basing yourself on what Amandro Riarixense says in his chronicle, because part of the province of Tarragona was named Catalonia by the Goths and the Alans, as most Spanish authors also say, ancient as well as modern, so that Otger got his name from the province, and not the province from Otger, as was the Romans' practice. And you've quoted sources for all of this which have left me perfectly satisfied.

Now I understand a lot of things about this principality that I'd never heard about before, and it's been a great pleasure. However, I haven't quite managed to grasp what you know about Catalonia's earliest institutions, with those nine lineages, in imitation of the nine choirs of angels, that it's said Charlemagne himself ordained and that King Louis of France, his son, created.[76] It looks to me as if you ran through all of that like a cat on hot coals. As it was such an extraordinary business, I wouldn't want it to be treated so lightly. I'd just like to ask you to tell Fabio and myself everything you know and think about it. We'd be delighted to hear it.

LIVIO: The carelessness of the Catalan nation when it comes to writing down and preserving things to do with Catalonia is so great that there's nothing like it to be seen anywhere. So it's hardly surprising that the people of Tortosa have allowed so many of the eminent distinctions that I've talked about simply to get lost and forgotten about. As they're Catalans, too, it's inevitable that the pots resemble the pans. That's why I shan't be able to satisfy you very much as regards what you're asking me. Still, I'll do what I can, and I'll tell you with pleasure what I know. However, as you're forcing me to do it, I'm confident that you'll pay me well. Since Luke the Evangelist says that "The labourer deserves his wages" — and the price could be a really good horse that Don Pedro could send me from Valencia! — it's fair enough that I make an effort to comply with your wishes, and I'll do my best. However, before I actually tell you everything I know — which in truth isn't much because, as I've said, not much has been written about it — I'll first explain the reasons why there's so little written evidence about the many heroic deeds that were performed in Spain in the earliest times.

First, it's because the Catalan language hasn't got the same abundance of words and terms that Latin possesses to express easily and elegantly whatever anyone might wish to say, even though the ones it has got are extremely effective... Also Latin, which could have remedied that lack, wasn't learned by many people in the olden days, because they didn't value learning as much then as when the Romans were at the height of their power. That's why we don't find many of the things that the Catalans accomplished written about, which is why we can truly state that the Catalans have always been men of

---

[76] As Livio explains shortly, according to legend, Otger, known as the 'Pare de la Pàtria' (Father of the Nation), persuaded the Nine Knights, or Barons, to swear to free Catalonia from Muslim occupation. The legend is thought to have been created in the Middle Ages with a view to consolidating the prestige of the nine noble families involved.

works, rather than words, which is the opposite of the Castilians, who've always had more words than works to their name.

Secondly, because they say, and I've read it myself, that in King James' reign the royal archives in Barcelona were burnt down, and lots of manuscripts of chronicles and other important documents were destroyed. That's where, no doubt, the little that had been written about the oldest times was to be found, including what you're asking about concerning Catalonia's original institutions. In fact, that was one of the worst disasters to have befallen Catalonia. That's why we wander about half blind when it comes to things to do with this principality, especially things concerning the conquest begun by the Nine Barons and by Charlemagne. You can find records of episodes that happened earlier, because more trustworthy and authoritative Latin and Greek authors wrote about them. It's undoubtedly an odd thing, and a great shame, that we know more about earlier events than about later ones.

Getting back to the point, namely that business about the nine lineages, what I say is that I believe for certain that what they say about them is perfectly true, and for the following three reasons. First and foremost, because in Catalonia we actually find and see all the houses of those nine lineages still surviving — the Nine Barons, the Nine Counts, the Nine Viscounts, the Nine Nobles and the Nine *Varvassors*[77] — and, that being so, if we didn't believe in them, we'd be denying the evidence of our own eyes. Secondly, given that the original chronicles of those events can't be found because, as I've said, they were probably destroyed in that fire at the royal archives, what *can* be found is summaries or abbreviated versions of those works made by Tomic, by Lucio Marineo and, most recently, by Don Jeroni Sans, abbot of Benifassà, as well as other old works, all of which amply record those nine lineages without a shadow of doubt. In particular, I've read some — and I've got copies of them — that were written two hundred years ago, although the name of the compiler isn't known, and they've never been printed. Whilst in many other respects they differ from the writings of Tomic and Lucio Marineo, as far as the earliest institutions of Catalonia are concerned, including the business of the nine lineages, they're very close — they hardly diverge one iota — and it seems clear that the authors wouldn't have

---

77 This term is explained, a little further on, by Livio.

written what they wrote if they hadn't found it written at greater length elsewhere. There's nothing odd or new about writing summaries, and there's nothing new about people according them the same credibility as would be due to the original works. We haven't got the original versions of Livy's *Decades*, or of Pompeius Trogus' great opus, but that doesn't stop us trusting the summaries that we've got of their works — the first done by Florus, the second by Justin. We trust their summaries as much as we'd trust the original authors.

If anyone said that the authors of the digests or summaries — it's all the same — that talk about things to do with Catalonia don't say which authors they take them from, as Florus and Justin do, I'd reply that they *do* say that what they were writing was summaries of the chronicles of Catalonia, which is all they *can* say, because those chronicles weren't written by a single author, as was the case of Livy for Florus, or Pompeius Trogus for Justin, but by several different authors, because each king had one or two or more chroniclers, and those writers who later decide to make summaries of everything they find written at length in those chronicles don't usually mention their sources. It's good enough if they just make brief mention of the princes and their doings. It's the opposite of what one needs to do if one just wants to summarise a single author, if that author deals at length with different periods. That's why I reckon it's good enough for Tomic and others to have summarised what they found, without needing to say exactly what they were summarising. Because not even Livy in his *Decades*, or Josephus in his *In antiquitatibus*, or Plutarch in his *In vita illustrium*, or Berossus in his *In monarquia caldeorum*, or any number of other authors in everything they wrote — which is lots and lots of hundreds, and even thousands — say what their sources were. They just say what they've read or discovered some other way, trying to reach the truth as best they can, in accordance with the ideas they find. Well, then, getting back to those nine lineages we were talking about, those ideas are as clear as they could possibly be, because, as I say, we see before our very eyes what we read in documents, and we also know that, when a king makes a knight a baron in this principality, what he says is that he gives him the very same authority and pre-eminence as are possessed by any of the Nine Barons of Catalonia. Isn't that a convincing enough argument?

DON PEDRO: It's so convincing that I reckon it's as good as proof.

Livio: That's it. And the third and final reason is that the general and universal opinion regarding this principality — what people think and believe — has always been, and still is, without the slightest shadow of doubt, that the business of those nine lineages came about just as all those writers I've named say. That's why it's reckless on the part of Carbonell to dare to state and affirm that the business of the nine lineages isn't true, in the face of the authority of so many hundreds of years since they were established and the general belief that holds them to be such, without counting, as I've said, what Tomic and the rest write, because it's obvious that they based their writings on older sources, who may well have taken the information from the original documents before they were burnt, or they may even have taken it themselves directly from the originals, as I believe to have been the case.

Tomic says that Filomena, Charlemagne's secretary, wrote about it in a chronicle that he composed on the emperor in the year 785, and he says the emperor ordered in his will that his son Louis should create the nine lineages and that Filomena was given the will. Those who have any doubts about that should just read Filomena, and they'll find the truth and the way it all came about. Some Catalan knights who, in their own interest, don't wish to admit the truth about the earliest institutions, treat Tomic as suspect and say that he wrote what he wrote about the nine lineages because he was a servant and follower of the house of Pinós, which was one of the Nine Worthy Barons. But, in fact, that point counts against them, rather than in their favour, because, if he'd written what he wrote about the nine lineages in order to honour that family, as they claim, he'd have put it first amongst those nine, and he'd have been justified in doing so, as the house of Pinós is so important and illustrious in Catalonia. But, not only didn't he put it first — he didn't even name it as head of one of those groups of three, even though he mentions the Montcadas, the Cerveras and the Anglesolas as heads and founders of those groups, as indeed they were, whereas he put the Pinóses in second place in the first of those groups, as did all the other authors who'd written about this, hundreds of years before he did, at least as far as the chronicles are concerned, and I reckon they were written a hundred years before Tomic. Even though they differ on many points, as I've said, they're very much in agreement about the earliest institutions.

And Lucio Marineo doesn't write as sparingly about the nine lineages as you might think, but does so in quite a complimentary way. Referring to them, he says: "*Quas fuerint a multis aliis enarratas*", which means they'd been written about a lot, and he goes on to say: "*anno christianae salutis DCCXXXIII*", by which he shows quite clearly that a lot of people had written about the nine lineages. And the reason Carbonell gives for his view — not just contradicting Tomic, but actually insulting him — is really very weak and unsupported, as all he says is that he'd never come across or read anything about it. And, just because he'd never read or come across anything, it doesn't follow that it never happened, because it's quite possible that the original documents were in the royal archives and that he didn't look for them hard enough, or else that they were unfortunately amongst the papers that got burnt, or were lost in some other way. The fact that they can't be found in our day doesn't prove that they were never there, as it's impossible to prove a negative in a case like that. But Carbonell was as bad at looking into this as in looking into what Pomponius Mela wrote about the word Tulcis, which, as I told you, is in fact the name of a river, whereas he says it's Tortosa. Because he's so careless about what he says, he's created such confusion regarding the admirable business of the nine lineages that he's split Catalonia into two warring parties over the issue. And I don't see why he's done it. If the creation of the lineages were prejudicial, or dimmed the lustre of Catalonia, there'd be no harm denying it, even if there were no good grounds for that. But, as it's such an important and singular fact, indeed one that's unique in the whole of Christendom, I don't understand what could have persuaded him to deny it, as he does, especially with him being a Catalan. A Castilian couldn't have done worse. And it's gross impertinence and audacity on Carbonell's part to claim, in respect of Filomena, who's quoted by Tomic, that there's no such author to be found. In fact, it's a bit thick of him to say that, just because he'd never seen or heard his name, he could never have existed. In that respect, Carbonell shows that he's just as conceited as a certain doctor of laws who, when another doctor with whom he was in dispute cited a certain ordinance, had the cheek to reply: "In truth, no such law is to be found in the entire legal system."[78] But everyone can believe whatever they like. As I say, I'll never be persuaded to believe that the whole busi-

[78] In the original, the quotation is in Latin.

ness didn't happen just as we find it described and approved by the weight of so many hundreds of years that it's been held to be true.

And I'm even more amazed by what Don Alonso d'Erill told me here in Tortosa, when he was accompanying the count of Aitona, about the Aragonese Jerónimo Zurita, who's writing a great history of Spain, and in particular of the Crown of Aragon, but doesn't intend to mention the immense distinction of those nine lineages, because he too says he hasn't found any original documents that refer to them.[79] And he's wrong to omit them, for the reasons I've already explained. And, if I see him before he finishes his work, I'll insist that on no account should he leave them out.

FABIO: It's very proper indeed that you do that, and I beg you, as a Catalan, to do it, so that so special a fact as the nine lineages doesn't just fall into oblivion.

DON PEDRO: As far as I'm concerned, all I can say is that, either I'm too soft and credulous, or else the force of your arguments has convinced me. I'm certain that your opinion about the nine lineages is correct and that what Carbonell says is absurd, or, as you say, pure folly and ignorance. I think you need to be believed when it comes to this, because your family isn't one of the nine, so no-one can say that you're moved by self-interest. I'm satisfied about what I asked you to explain — and I hope you will be, too, with the horse that you asked me to send you! The only thing I'd still like to know is what *Varvassor* means, and where the title comes from, as I've never heard it mentioned except here in Catalonia.

LIVIO: Varvassors are the same as "The town gates, or upright defences of the realm." That's what Oberto Dall'Orto and Niccolò Baldo say, and then they go on to explain: "And these were were once called chieftains among the Lombards."[80]

DON PEDRO: Very good! I'm pleased to hear it. And now, let's go onto the bridge, and we can keep on talking as we walk. There we'll be out in the open. Even though the exits by the Vimpeçol Gate and Temple Gate are fine, Bridge Gate has the advantage that it takes you right onto the sea, as well as the land, as the river is so wide and mighty here that it looks as if it could actually be the sea.

79 The first of the six volumes of Jerónimo de Zurita's *Anales de la Corona de Aragón* was published in 1562.

80 In the original, both quotations are in Latin. *Varvassor* is, in fact, said to come from Medieval Latin *vassus vassorum*, or vassal of vassals, the latter referring to the great noblemen of Catalonia.

FABIO: Although the river here is so wide and strong, on occasion it's been frozen over and didn't flow at all.

DON PEDRO: You must be joking! That's impossible!

FABIO: No, I'm telling the truth, believe me! In January 1506 it froze right over, and the ice was so thick and hard that people walked across it perfectly safely, and so did a man riding a mule, and even he didn't come to grief. There are also records of it freezing over in 1442, on the eve of St. Lucy's Day, but that wasn't as serious as the last time.

LIVIO: There's no doubt that what Fabio says did happen. The astonishing thing is that it can happen here, where the earth is so warm. In Germany rivers freeze over every year, even those that are as big as this one, or even bigger, but what makes that happen is that the earth gets extremely cold up there, because they're so far north.

DON PEDRO: I know that's so, but it's really amazing that it could happen here, because the land here is as temperate as in Valencia, and I know that because I've eaten cherries as early in the year here as down there.

LIVIO: Be that as it may, that's what happens. Do you see how fast those boats are casting their nets, one after the other, to fish shad?

FABIO: The fish must be biting, there are so many of them.

DON PEDRO: Is it only shad that they fish?

FABIO: Sometimes they catch sturgeon and lamprey, but that way of fishing is for shad.

LIVIO: Would you like to have a go at *peda*, Don Pedro? You'd enjoy it.

DON PEDRO: What do you mean by *peda*?

LIVIO: Every time the fishermen cast a net, they call it a *peda*.

DON PEDRO: And where does the word *peda* come from?

LIVIO: From the verb *repedo, repedas*, which comes from *pedo, pedas*, which means repeating the same interval or distance on a path or a road, as those men who fish shad do in the river. As you can see, when they've cast their nets once, they do it again, and they never stop coming and going, day and night, but without ever going further away from the original spot.

FABIO: My goodness, what a fitting word that is! I thought it had been chosen at random, or just by whim.

LIVIO: Well, you can see that it wasn't. It was chosen for good reason.

DON PEDRO: Let's go and cast a net, then! When we're in the boat, we'll be able to talk even better than here, and we'll be able to see from close up how they catch the shad. What a very special treat this is! There's nothing like it anywhere! There's no doubt about it — you've got a lot more things than you realise.

LIVIO: We know there isn't another river in Spain that gives as much pleasure and profit, and there aren't any outside Spain that can better it, either. As regards pleasure, there are all those fresh, clear springs to be found by its side, all those channels and cool groves and gardens on its banks where we go and enjoy ourselves in the summer. I don't think there's a better place in the world for men or women to enjoy and amuse themselves, because you can go boating without getting exhausted. As regards profit, just think of the number of different kinds of excellent fish that can be caught here, and the trade that creates.

DON PEDRO: Yes, I believe that's the case. They tell me the fishing industry here is something tremendous. Is the fish all caught in the river?

FABIO: Holy Mary, no! What's caught in the river is lamprey, shad, sturgeon and eel, which compete with the mullet, grey mullet, leaping mullet, sea bass, barbel and nase.

DON PEDRO: The first three you mention are extremely delicious. I don't think there's anything to compare with them in the sea.

LIVIO: That's what lots of people think, but you can't lay down rules when it comes to taste.

FABIO: That's true, because, as far as I'm concerned, I like prawns more than any of those others that you've mentioned.

DON PEDRO: Oh, they're very special! Particularly the ones they catch here. There's no doubt about it — they're better than anywhere else. Do they actually fish them in the river?

FABIO: Not at all. The prawns, sole, brill, bream, oyster, red mullet, tuna, leerfish, sea bass, croaker, and innumerable other kinds of fish come from the sea and from lagoons, and the best thing about them is that each species, one after the other, has its own season, like fruit.

DON PEDRO: I don't quite follow.

FABIO: What I'm saying is that, although you can eat any fish all the year round, each kind is at its best in its own season — like sea bream, mullet, eel, sole and garfish, between St. Michael's Day and Christmas; sea bass, grey mullet, shad, hake and tuna, from Christmas to Lent; lamprey, shad, sturgeon, pandora, brill and tuna, from Lent till May; steenbras, horse mackerel, mackerel, grey mullet, red mullet, cuttlefish and pilchard, from May to St. John's; sea bass, croaker, leerfish and golden mullet, from St. John's till the Assumption; and leaping mullet, conger, white sea bream, dentex, moray and a fish we call the *morrotrony*, from the Assumption to St. Michael's. There are other kinds of fish that are just as good at any time of the year, like prawns, oysters, shrimps, mussels, clams, wedge shells, nutshells, crab, octopus, shamefaced crab, squid, grouper, and lots of others that I don't recall.

DON PEDRO: What amazing things these are! I say it's a fact that there's no place like this anywhere under the sun. But I suppose the fish that's caught in the lagoons isn't as good as the rest. At least, that's the case with the fish that's caught in the Albufera, in Valencia, which must be much like your lagoons here.

FABIO: No, they're really excellent, because the sea generally flows in and out of those lagoons, and the rainwater can't flow back or be held in reservoirs, as happens in the Albufera. If you saw the tackle and the equipment that the fishermen here use when they go fishing, and the number of different ways they fish, and all the different names they have for their gear, you'd be astonished. First, there's a long net they call a *brogina*, the queen of all fishing gear, which can be a thousand yards long. It's so massive that just one, in a single sweep, can catch over a thousand baskets of fish, and each basket holds up to roughly a hundredweight. They also use sweep nets, dragnets, drift nets, gillnets, cast nets, hand nets and shad nets for the lagoons and for the river, and fyke nets, trawl-lines for sea bass and eels, lave nets, purse nets, harpoons, traps, stake nets, eel bucks, basket traps, fykes, cuttlefish traps, hand nets, sturgeon troughs, and what we call *arcinals, camallocs* and *ventoles*. With all that tackle they can fish at sea, in the lagoons and on the river.

DON PEDRO: That was quite a litany! They must be extremely expert.

FABIO: There aren't any fishermen on the whole of the Spanish coast as skilful as those from Tortosa.

DON PEDRO: So how come they say that the most expert fishermen come from Tarragona?

FABIO: That's what they say, but it's nonsense. All you need do is compare the enormous number of different kinds of tackle that are used here and the very few kinds that are used up there, and you can see the difference right away. There all they use is fyke nets, sweep nets, trawl lines, *arcinals,* and I don't know what else, because in Tarragona the only place they can fish is in the sea, whereas here, as I say, we can fish in the sea, in the lagoons and on the river, and each of them requires different kinds of tackle.

Don Pedro: Your answer is perfectly clear. But tell me, in those lagoons or lakes of yours, and on the river banks and meadows, are there any birds that can be hunted with shotguns or bows and arrows, as in the Albufera?

Fabio: There's an infinite number! It's almost impossible to imagine. And telling you their names would involve another litany, no shorter than the one I gave you just now! First of all, there are swans, flamingos, coots, Sardinian and French geese, ducks, pintails, tufted ducks, crested grebes, cormorants, bitterns — these last scared away King John's army at Amposta — puffins, lapwings, plovers, curlews, swamp hens, night herons, common moorhens, grey herons, purple herons, little egrets, brown herons, cattle egrets, great egrets, seagulls, sparrow hawks, stone curlews and terns, as well as what we call *cabirois, periçons, esclaus, movietes* and *eixadells.* And there are also ospreys and skuas, two birds of prey that hunt in really strange ways. The ospreys dive down and catch the fish in flight; and the skuas fly after the gulls, not to kill them but to eat their droppings, pursuing and harassing the poor things so hard that, out of pure fright, they make them excrete in the air, and they eat it in full flight, and that's what the skuas live on.

Don Pedro: Well, that's really amusing. Those birds are certainly dirty hunters. Their prey can't be terribly sought after!

Fabio: I want to tell you something else about the great abundance of birds that breed on these banks, and it's so very strange that I'm afraid you just won't believe it. It really happens like this, because I've had it confirmed by honest fishermen, and they've all said the same thing. And it's this. A few years ago, quite by chance, some fishermen found a nest where some birds similar to those were breeding — they were flamingos, which are a little smaller than cranes — and there were so many eggs there that they could have filled the boat in which they usually carry fish back here to Tortosa, and the boat can take fifty hundredweight.

Don Pedro: Can that possibly be true?

Fabio: It's absolutely true. The fishermen took eight or ten basketsful, as they didn't want any more, and they left the rest there.

Don Pedro: Even if it's true, I wouldn't dare repeat it anywhere else.

FABIO: The marvellous things to be found here are so many that we either just have to talk about them like this, or else we need to carry certificates around to prove them! Well, if you saw and enjoyed the pleasures and the pastimes that are to be had by the shore over there, with all the different kinds of hunting, you'd be no less astounded than by all the different kinds of fishing. First of all, we hunt wild boar on horseback, and, as the boar defend themselves, it's a veritable skirmish. I regard that as the most real kind of hunt to be found anywhere. We also hunt them in a different way, by having them thrown into the river and then attacking them from boats and spearing them — that's the most amusing kind of hunt there is for ladies. And we also catch them by waiting for them on the paths that they use. As for the deer, we kill them by startling them and then catching them in nets, and by waiting for them down by the river, like the boar. That's what happens on the shore, but those sorts of game, and lots of others, also live up in the mountains, and there they're hunted differently. Actually, what with the plains and the mountains, there's so much game that there's hardly a day in the week that the butchers' shops here don't stock game meat, whether it's boar, goat or deer. And down by the shore there are masses of rabbit and hare, and perfect land on which to hunt. More than twenty hare have been killed, and more than fifty rabbits, on a single day. And there's excellent falconry for hunting game birds, such as cranes, great egrets, grey and purple herons, little egrets, brown herons, curlews, cattle egrets, and lots more, and for goshawks, francolins, partridges and owls. In fact, there's no end to the number of marvels and wonders to be found on the shore. We even find enormous quantities of pond turtles and Caspian turtles, and a thousand other lesser creatures, which is quite amazing. If only you could see how we get the fishing tackle and the gear ready, you'd be dumbfounded. We get into our boats and go hunting along the entire shore, which is enormously long, going from one lagoon to another, and into the irrigation channels, and never having to get out on land. At every moment there's something or other to catch, at every instant you can see lots of different ways of fishing.

And, if you want cattle, there's as much here as anywhere on earth, because we breed innumerable flocks of sheep and we fatten yearlings on those salty pastures. They're fit for a king. If you go up there hungry, all you need do is put your feet down on the earth and there isn't any kind of food that won't thrill you. Even if it isn't the very top quality, up there you'll eat it with more appetite than the very best food you can get down here. It's a veritable Promised Land! There's nothing anywhere on earth to compare with its delights.

DON PEDRO: Before you've finished, you'll be making me take a detour to go and enjoy all the marvellous things you've been telling me about.

FABIO: For sure, you mustn't miss going to see it, either now or else on your way back home.

DON PEDRO: Just leave it to me. I'll take care of it. They tell me you've also got lots of farms around here with all kinds of cattle and that you cultivate an astonishing number of different kinds of fruit — so many that it's more than some whole kingdoms produce.

FABIO: What you've been told is perfectly true. We've got so many things here that you'll be just as amazed when you hear about them as you've been by what you've heard already. First of all, we've got wheat. Even if it isn't as much as we need, we can easily obtain enough for ourselves, because we can get it by river from Urgell and Aragon, and from the Ports de Morella,[81] which is like a second Urgell and isn't far away. And, in the last resort, there's always the sea. And then we've got barley and other lesser crops, such as hemp and linen, and seeds for sowing onions and cabbages which are so special that they're exported everywhere, especially if they're from the vegetable gardens at Pimpí. And we've got no end of olive oil — it's as plentiful as wheat in Urgell, and it's the best in Europe. And very good wines, especially the clarets. And then figs, carobs, honey and wax, any amount of fish, saltwort for soap, glasswort for glass, madderwort for red dyes, redoul for tanning, dyer's weed for yellow dyes, salt in great quantities, hugely increasing silk production, masses of wood — the best, or at least the strongest, in Spain. And then tar, pitch, turpentine, charcoal, long-burning firewood, massive numbers of palm trees — fan palms which, once they've been sawn, are loaded onto ships, as well as plenty of very good real palms — and esparto, which, although there isn't much of it, is very tough. There's also high quality gypsum for house building, and in my time I've seen it sold at only eight shillings a bushel, which would be sixpence for one of your Valencian bushels. There's also very good gypsum for use in winemaking.

---

81 The 'Ports of Morella' are the mountains around the city of Morella.

Then we've got dairy farms, plenty of excellent horse breeding stables, as well as sheep and goats, and the quality of the land is excellent for them to winter here. In the winter they practically cover the shore. In fact, there have been years when eighty thousand head have come to winter in this area. The wool of some of the animals that are native to the area is as fine as that in Castile, and they use it to make the very lightest of cloths. There are piggeries, too, and lots of very good flocks of goats. And, on top of all that, we've got the river trade, which is extremely important, and it's invaluable for the ports of Alfacs and Ampolla, which are by the sea and in our district.

In addition, as far as things that are pleasing to the taste and the eye are concerned, we've got all kinds of citrus fruits in great abundance: citrons, limes, Cetalia lemons and common lemons, oranges and grapefruit, and the trees are trained to form delicious arbours, covered in greenery, which it's a glory to behold. And then we've got lots of other good and tasty produce — infinite amounts of capers, samphire and dwarf palms; and extraordinary perfumed waters, such as orange blossom water, rose water, musk rose water, clover water, myrtle water and others. In particular, they manufacture so much orange blossom water that it supplies half of Aragon. And then there are cordials, made from arbutus fruit, sorrel, endives, Italian bugloss, sage, eyewort, rosemary, basil, borage, compass weed, and an incredible number of others. I can tell you this: the different herbs that are good for your health and used by apothecaries and grow around here are so numerous that you can find here practically all the ones that grow anywhere in Spain, including sarsaparilla, which is used to treat syphilis, and also serpent root.

DON PEDRO: God save my soul! I'm absolutely astonished by what you say. Is it possible that so many things can be found within the bounds of one small city?

FABIO: Although the city is small now, its boundaries are very large. It's nine Catalan leagues long, and seven wide.

DON PEDRO: What? It can't possibly be that big! There isn't a city in all these kingdoms, or at least in the three main ones, that's half that size!

LIVIO: It's just as Fabio says. There's no question about it.

FABIO: Yes, and it's so well adorned and furnished with manor houses that it's just glorious to go for walks and look at it. The fact is you can find over three hundred manors and farmsteads within the Tortosa district, and there are plenty of very beautiful fortified towers, and lots of their estates are so important that I don't know if you'd believe me.

DON PEDRO: Say whatever you like. I don't think it will be any more incredible than what you've told me already!

FABIO: It may seem incredible, but it's true all the same. There's one, above all, that produces huge quantities of cereals. It's called L'Aldea, and it belongs to Ramon Jordà. They harvest nearly two thousand bushels of grain, in Tortosa measures — that's to say some three thousand Urgell bushels, or more than five thousand Valencian ones. There's another one that's famous for its olive oil that's called Xalamera and belongs to the friars of Benifassà. They produce over one thousand three hundred pitchers of oil. There's another that's known for its carobs. It belongs to Pere Sevil, and they harvest over two thousand hundredweight. There's yet another estate, called La Torre de Llaber. It belongs to Cristòfol Despuig,[82] and it grows several kinds of produce: olive trees that give four hundred pitchers of oil, carob trees that give four hundred hundredweight of nuts, a plantation of mulberry trees that gives two pounds of seed, and fig trees that give a hundredweight of figs, and it's all increasing rapidly. There's also rich fertile soil which produces a hundred and fifty bushels of wheat, and some good sheep folds. And, believe me, there are plenty more like that, and just as good, in the area, though I've only mentioned four, just to give you an idea, and each one of them has its own distinctive features. From what I've told you about them, you can imagine how important the rest of them are.

DON PEDRO: It's so very extraordinary that I can't think of anything like it. Each of them sounds more like a whole district than an estate. I guess there can't be many places in Catalonia that are as productive for their owners as these are here.

LIVIO: There's no doubt about it. And the area has got another special feature, too. It seems strange to me, and it will surprise you as much as everything else. Within the city bounds — in fact within two leagues — it's got the two extremes of early and late fruits. That's to say, in one part, which is down here by the shore where we are, fruit is harvested as early as in Valencia, and in the other part, in the mountains in front of us, where they gather firewood, it's harvested as late as up in the sierra.

---

[82] I.e. the author of the *Dialogues*.

DON PEDRO: It certainly is wonderful that in one small area you can find as much as you'd expect to find in a whole kingdom. I've never heard of such a thing in my life. Because of that, and all the other many and varied things it boasts, it would be perfectly proper to call it a *microbasilia*,[83] which means a world in miniature. And are those mountains up there the ones where the king ordered the trees, which are said to be so special, to be cut down to make galleys?

FABIO: Yes, those are the ones. And the truth is that the wood is so excellent that there's none better to be found anywhere, and it's used to make ships of all kinds, as well as royal galleys. The king's admirals say there's nothing like them. All the trees grown up there are very special, and the villages around here use them to make all sorts of products. The land on those heights is so open and fresh that cattle can pasture there in the summer, just as well as in the mountains. Amongst all the other excellent things we've got, this is one of the best — that within the city bounds we've got refuge for the cattle in summer, as well as in winter, which is what you might expect to find in a whole kingdom. It's so healthy up there that we're all amazed that our ancestors didn't build houses there to get away from the heat in the summer down here by the shore. It would have been a very salutary idea.

DON PEDRO: Do you mean those mountains are so special, and there are so many comfortable spots to be found there, that that would actually be feasible?

FABIO: What do you mean by "so special"? Yes, they're so special that, if I started going into detail, I'd plunge straight into an abyss as huge as any of the previous ones.

DON PEDRO: Well, let's have it all, since we've started on the subject.

FABIO: First of all, up there you can find the most exquisite water on earth in the clearest and freshest of springs. In particular, there's one — the Font Cendrosa — which is so extraordinary that it would astonish you. Every Friday and Saturday the water there comes up so cloudy and mixed up with ash that it looks as if it's been stirred up inside a cauldron full of cinders, and every other day of the week it's as clear as sunlight. Up there you can find most of the herbs that apothecaries use. And there's an infinite number of sweet-smelling alpine flowers and all sorts of woodland fruits. There are even chestnut trees.

---

[83] Based on ancient Greek *basileia*, meaning a kingdom.

LIVIO: Chestnuts! I didn't know that.

FABIO: There are chestnut trees at Carles — not very many, but there are some. And if you wanted to take the time to sow or plant chestnuts up there, I'm certain they'd do as well there as anywhere else. The trees that grow there are splendid: stone pine, black pine, Aleppo pine, Portuguese oak, holm oak, Italian maple, wild service — these last two being excellent for chair making —, whitebeam, lime, elder, beech, yew, box, snowy mespilus, Italian buckthorn, terebinth, strawberry tree, green and wild juniper, hawthorn, hazelnut, holly — out of which they make birdlime —, ash, cypress, Phoenician juniper, and a tree we call *ratabosc*. Besides, it's such a fertile mountain that it produces a thousand different kinds of largesse, especially wild mushrooms, of which there are such quantities, and so many different species, that it's simply wonderful — lactarius, brittlegill, wood mushroom, waxcap mushrooms, glutinous waxcaps, pinkmottle woodwax, grey knight, coral fungus, morel, summer truffle, gilded brittlegill, charcoal burner, chanterelle, and yellow foot. All of them are excellent to eat, whereas there are some that aren't edible but can be used for other purposes — red russula, devil's mushroom, stem bolete — and you can also find truffles, because every kind of mushroom can be found up there. There's also extremely fine red clay, jet, mercury, iron mines, and one of the best places for a foundry to be found anywhere.

DON PEDRO: Why don't they build one there, then?

FABIO: For the same reason that they don't do other things that would be really practical and beneficial for the city. In those mountains there's also plenty of wildlife — a lot more than down here on the plain — like wild boar, deer, mountain goats, roe-deer, martens, genets, badgers, servals, squirrels, rabbits, hare and *arrions*, and they're much bigger than down here by the river. And the two great nightmare animals are to be found there, too — wolves and foxes — just to make sure that people don't forget to protect and take care of their animals and poultry. And lots of birds of prey breed there, such as the golden eagle, black hawk-eagle, buzzard, snake eagle, falcon, goshawk, merlin, hobby and sparrow hawk. And you can catch trout, eel, barbel and nase.

And, finally, there's the shape and the layout of the land. Everyone still believes, as they did in the olden days, that there are gold and silver deposits up there, and it's known that at one time people went prospecting for them. If they didn't find any, it was because the time wasn't ripe, as it has been in other parts of Spain, where plenty of both metals is mined. I can assure you that in one part of this area, called the valley of Rubí, you can find precious stones, such as rubies, jacinths, emeralds and garnets, and there must be plenty of them, if only people bothered to look for them. I remember hearing Miquel Domènec, who ran an inn in La Cruera Street, tell how an Italian jewel dealer used to come and stay there every year and then go off with a bagful of stones which, when they were cut, produced gems. And a few years ago Mateu Mauri, the huntsman, used to tell how one day in that very valley, when he was stalking a deer, it started raining and he went and sheltered in a little cave, and how from there he saw stones shining, as I think the water makes them shine, and, not thinking much about it, he took a few, which a silversmith called Master Bernat the Hunchback bought from him for a few coins, and when he'd cut them he sold them for a lot of money. That's true. And there are other ways, too, in which people have learned that there are plenty of precious stones around these parts.

DON PEDRO: I can tell you it's a great business. What you're telling me is amazing. If I didn't know you told the truth — and seeing how you're talking about local matters about which you can find out everything there is to know — I'd find it really hard to believe you.

FABIO: What I've been saying about the excellence of the whole of this area is exactly as I've been telling you. And there are other things, too, that I'm bound to be forgetting. But everything I've said is fact.

DON PEDRO: In short, if you had kermes dye, sugar and rice, as we have in the kingdom of Valencia, and if your mares produced good quality horses, you'd have absolutely everything.

FABIO: The horses we breed aren't bad. In fact, they're as good, or nearly as good, as those in Castile, but I can tell you for certain that, if all the owners of the mares used good horses as sires — as, in fact, most of them do — and followed the regulations that they apply in Castile, we'd produce horses just as good as there and we wouldn't need to go to Castile for horses. Instead we could supply the whole of Catalonia, because our individual mares are very well shaped and they have a docile temperament, and the land here is very suitable for pack animals, and the grass is good for them, in summer as well as winter, and the climate is temperate. I've heard people who know about these things say it's as good here as in Andalusia.

DON PEDRO: I'm surprised, then, that they don't do it. Why doesn't the king command it? Wouldn't the fact that the whole kingdom could be supplied be reason enough?

LIVIO: Maybe one day that will happen.

FABIO: As for the rest of what you've been saying, Don Pedro, we've got kermes dye here and, if we did things properly and carefully, we'd be able to produce quite a lot of that uncommon substance. And sugar could be, and actually has been, refined in Xerta, a village that's within the city's jurisdiction, and I've seen the moulds into which they poured it. Older people in the village remember seeing other pieces of apparatus, and it's been shown that sugar cane does very well here. Mossèn Miquel Terçà, whom I've mentioned before, had some sugar cane planted by his tower, or castle, of Burjassénia, which is an excellent estate, and also on another enclosed estate of his, in front of us here, and it did very well in both places. So, if only we had a sugar mill, we'd be in business. I can tell you that the best equipment is in Xerta, and it's the most obvious place there is for it, because the land is irrigated and well sheltered from north and north-westerly winds, and it faces south, so it's very warm, and the soil is superb. True, there aren't any rice fields here, as we haven't got an irrigation scheme, but there's land and space enough down by the coast that's as good as any anywhere. If God wills that the irrigation system that was started down by the dam — which is where most of the shad and lamprey and sturgeon are caught — is finished, we'll have everything that's needed in great plenty, and lots more besides.

DON PEDRO: I'm told that the works down by the dam are an excellent beginning — splendid and very safe, which is what matters with projects like that. Why isn't that work being carried on, seeing how useful and profitable it would be for the city?

FABIO: I just don't know the answer to that one — at least none that's of any use. Maybe Livio can help.

LIVIO: I can't help you, either. I reckon God has decided that its time just hasn't yet come, in the same way as with the mines, and that must be because we're all sinners, as I can't think of any other explanation. We can see the project's possibilities with our own eyes, we can see what a really fine start was made on it, we can understand how immensely beneficial it would be, and we know how many thousands

of ducats it's cost us. It's obvious that nothing's been more sorely neglected than that ill-starred undertaking. It's plain blindness, it's simple stupidity, and I can't help saying that it's the greatest misfortune
that's ever been seen. It almost feels as if those people who are preventing the completion of as an important project as that were committing an act of treachery on this poor city. Let those people listen
who wish to hear and want to understand — if they hope to convince
anyone that in the end the project won't be required, they're utterly mistaken. Sooner or later, the irrigation scheme will be completed by order of the city or the king, or by those who obtain his authorisation. What bothers me and weighs heavily on my soul is the idea
that we could have it right now and reap the benefit from it in our day,
instead of putting it off because we listened to what the enemies of
the common good advised. The city really ought to consider that this
isn't the time to abandon the work, seeing the state it's reached,
because, if it's left as it is, it's perfectly obvious that we'll have thrown
away those seven thousand shillings that have recently been invested in it. What needs to be done is what men do who, when they go out
hunting, lose an arrow and then shoot another to recover the first
one. Saying there's no way to carry out the job is no excuse, because
it's been judged to be very beneficial, both for the community and for
the individuals who make it up. But I don't see it being supported or
resolved — just carped at and criticised.

FABIO: I've heard people say they've stopped building the irrigation
works because it would cost fifty thousand ducats or more, which you
can see is clearly way beyond the means of a city like Tortosa.

LIVIO: What would that matter? The land that was irrigated would be
worth a hundred and fifty thousand times more than it's worth now!
That's why I've said on innumerable occasions that it wouldn't be
spending money. If the works were completed, it would be an invest-
ment in the growth of our own assets, at many shillings per pound.
And I've just thought of something else. If our grandparents — who
built that splendid dam to draw water from the Ebro, a project that
people thought impossible at the time — came back and saw our neg-
ligence and cowardice in not having the guts or the enterprise to
carry on and complete what's still outstanding, when *they* took on and
completed the hardest and almost impossible part, what would they
say, and what on earth would they think of us? I think they'd disclaim
their parentage and say we weren't worthy of them. I've heard it said

that, when that magnificent dam project was being carried out, the city guilds tried to outdo each other, and all of them worked so hard that it looked as if they expected to achieve salvation through it. And when it was finished, seeing before their very eyes what they could scarcely believe, they sang a *Te Deum* and, at the tops of their voices, cried out: "Now the land will be free and rich!" That's what they said, not doubting for one moment that their children wouldn't rest until they'd finished the irrigation scheme, and there's nothing we've neglected more. Just think how truly great the city would become, if only it had proper irrigation, what with the water from the Ebro!

DON PEDRO: Yes, and I'm actually surprised that the city isn't bigger, even without irrigation, seeing all the qualities and quantities that you've been telling me about. I imagine there must be some secret natural reason for that, unless it's some sort of scourge. Did your ancestors say anything about that?

FABIO: What I've heard is that the growth of the city was held back by the stagnant waters that are left behind after storms in some parts of the area right in front of us, in Castellnou and Vila-roja. And I've heard people say that, if there are so many storms that the waters in those two places meet, which can happen because they're next to each other, that that almost always causes deadly fevers. I can tell you that I've seen that happen twice, and it was so pitiless that it could have been the plague, and they say that that was the cause. Especially in 1525 and 1547, the fevers were so awful that they destroyed the city, no less than the plague in 1520 and 1521 and in 1530. I've seen all those calamities befall the city in my time.

DON PEDRO: I can well believe that that's one of the causes, and it ought to be remedied, if possible. But I doubt whether it's the main reason why Tortosa hasn't grown more. Maybe you don't know of any others, but that one doesn't really satisfy me. I've thought hard about the problem many a time, speculating on why some towns are big without there being any real explanation for it, whilst others are small when they look as if they could be much bigger, as in this case. What's more, you can see cities that have been very big for hundreds of years and have then grown smaller, like Lleida, and others that used to be small and are now very big, such as Barcelona, even though the area around Lleida is no worse than it used to be, and the area around Barcelona is no better, and even though we don't know of any particular reason why the one should have shrunk so much, and the

other expanded. All of which makes me conclude — without wanting to pry into Nature's secrets, which in truth haven't affected those
two cities, because Nature's always the same, whereas the development of those two cities has been so very different and, as I've said, we
don't know about special cases — that those variations in prosperity
and adversity come about as they do simply because God wills it,
which is the best and the most fundamental and Catholic reason,
whereas any other reasons would be merely idle speculation.

LIVIO: I agree entirely with that in every way. We've got the proof right
in front of us. As you say, although Tortosa is the third largest city in
Catalonia in terms of population, it's so small, compared to what it
ought to be, that it's hardly anything. After all, what does a town need
in order to be great that Tortosa hasn't got? A good climate, a good
location, plenty of trade by sea, river and land, two seaports at the
same distance from the three main cities of the Crown of Aragon, as
well as from Majorca. And great quantities of pack animals, salt and
fish, even more kinds and quantities of fruit, great length and
breadth of territory, plenty of freedoms, thanks to its privileges —
and, even so, it's stayed as small as it is. What can the reason be except,
as Don Pedro says, that it's God's pleasure that it be so?

FABIO: Well then, if that's what pleases God, let it please us, too, and may
God preserve it thus, and may we live in it thus. And, since we lack
nothing that we need, let's not go looking for things we don't need,
because middling kinds of things last longer, and Tortosa has grown
so old, as Livio has demonstrated, just because it hasn't been too big.
Let's give thanks to God for what we are, and let's pray to His infinite
goodness that it be kept like that for us forever in His holy service,
and may He allow all its citizens to persevere in the Catholic Christian
religion until the Day of the Universal and General Judgement,
amen.

LIVIO: What with all the talking we've done, it's getting quite dark.
Before we get out of the boat, don't forget to take the dozen shad with
you that we've caught, as we'll be needing them.

DON PEDRO: I'd like at least two in a sandwich to take with me on my
journey tomorrow.

FABIO: That's a good idea. You don't find shad everywhere. As you're
so near your house, why don't you two just go on, and allow me to
retire to mine.

LIVIO: Stay and have a meal with Don Pedro.

FABIO: I can't. I've got some writing to do. There's business to transact. I'll be here early in the morning, as he insists on leaving. We'll keep Don Pedro company for a little way and we'll be able to tell him what's still left to explain about things to do with Tortosa—especially what prices are paid every year for the fish that's caught here, and the salt, and the pack animals, and the fruit. Don Pedro will be just as amazed by that as he's been by everything else he's heard.

DON PEDRO: By faith, as I'm here, I really need to know everything!

LIVIO: As you wish. I think it's an excellent idea!

Laus Deo optimo et maximo